WHY THE EDUCATION SYSTEM FAILED and E-COMMERCE RISE

Romeo Olivier

Founder and CEO of www.fastlanemarketing.co.uk

authorHOUSE

AuthorHouse™ UK
1663 Liberty Drive
Bloomington, IN 47403 USA

© *2019 Romeo Olivier. All rights reserved.*

No part of this book may be reproduced, stored in a retrieval system, or transmitted by any means without the written permission of the author.

Published by AuthorHouse 02/12/2019

ISBN: 978-1-7283-8458-0 (sc)
ISBN: 978-1-7283-8459-7 (e)

Print information available on the last page.

Any people depicted in stock imagery provided by Getty Images are models, and such images are being used for illustrative purposes only.
Certain stock imagery © Getty Images.

This book is printed on acid-free paper.

Because of the dynamic nature of the Internet, any web addresses or links contained in this book may have changed since publication and may no longer be valid. The views expressed in this work are solely those of the author and do not necessarily reflect the views of the publisher, and the publisher hereby disclaims any responsibility for them.

Dedication

I want to thank my family for encouraging me to chase my dream of becoming an entrepreneur. It took them years to understand me but in the end, they finally did.

Also, to my future wife, my shiny star; thanks for believing in me way before I did with tremendous moral support. You're special.

To my circle of friends, I love you all.

Contents

Dedication iii
Introduction vii

Chapter 1 ~Days of Little Beginning~ 1
 Arriving in Europe.. 2
 My love for football 6
 Problem with the School System 8

Chapter 2 ~Moving to a New City~ 10
 College (High School) 11
 The girl from library 16
 The head of Maths...17

Chapter 3 ~University~... 21
 Second year... 22

Chapter 4 ~Second Phase of Experience at University~................... 26
 Third year... 27
 Dissertation 28
 Effective communication 31

Chapter 5 ~Graduation~... 33
 Employment 33

Chapter 6 ~Another Job Calls~ 38
 Uncle and nephew talk 38

Chapter 7	~Trip to South Africa~	42
Chapter 8	~Hunger for More~	45
	Friends and family	45
	Unemployment made me rich	46
	Financial education	49
Chapter 9	~More Lessons of Wealth~	52
	A day out with a friend's dad	54
	It Was Time to Action	55
	Talk with a Doctor	60
Chapter 10	~Value~	62
Chapter 11	~From Hero to Zero~	64
Chapter 12	~Time to Take a Break~	66
Chapter 13	~Back to Europe~	69
Chapter 14	~It Finally Paid Off Once Again~	73
	Conclusion	74

INTRODUCTION

It took me two years to write a book that could have been written in less than twelve months. Do you see why procrastination is a dream killer my friend? But that's ok, cause I have a story to share and its worth reading. This book is going to look and analyse the education system that me, you and as well as other people went or still attend. Please read this book with an open mind as its written with all honesty. However, do not misunderstand the whole idea because this book does NOT in any way encourage you to skip school, college or university. I'm here to talk about the education system as a whole and not a particular school. I believe everyone should go to school, but the system behind schools has failed many people and sadly, it is still failing and killing dreams. Please continue reading.

You might wonder why this book is different than most books out there. Well, let me explain, this book is different because it cuts down the core of the education system and why doing business online is such an extreme advantage today. I promise I will not waste your time, for you have made the right choice for picking up this book to read as it will not only help you but those around you as well! I'm truly honoured. The education system is one of the subjects that everyone talks about vaguely without having the courage to expose the truth to the world. This book you're holding is an authentic revelation of the truth that has been hidden for years and has turned out to affect many people later in life. Many people wish they had a better education, better guidance, and a good practical mentor. This is why I'm here; please read this book with discernment because the information it contains inside will not only be useful today but, in many years to come. I was a victim of the poor education system, but I managed to overcome it with time by continuously educating myself and cultivating curiosity to discover my purpose in life. Hence, I am willing to share my story with you, so you can be aware of what goes around behind education institutions. Please do NOT read this book in lust expecting some sort of quick and easy answer to be revealed, there is nothing new under the sun, and I'm not a genius. Do NOT start protesting into schools, colleges or universities; that's NOT what this book is about as I do NOT encourage any violence of any kind or offensive behaviour. Let's pretend we know each other and let me take you on a journey with me.

Chapter 1

~Days of Little Beginning~

I was brought up in a middle-class family in the north side of Kinshasa, Democratic Republic of the Congo. My dad was a judge, and my mom was a working nurse. I'm the second born in my family. Our parents wanted us to be successful like any other parents would want for their children. My dad was a very strict person. I wouldn't say people feared him, but a lot of people gave him the respect that he deserved. He was always telling us that we were different, compared to other kids around the neighbourhood, and he wouldn't like his reputation as a judge to be mediocre. So, we all took that into consideration—apart from me. I was always a turbulent kid. As years went by, my auntie, who was working in the embassy of the Congo, had a plan to send me to Europe to study and have a better life in general. It was a big issue, as I had to be separate from my parents at a very young age. I was seven. My dad never agreed with it, because I was his only son. At the same time, it was a good opportunity for a better life. My mother also loved me so much to the point where she kept persuading my dad that it was for the best. As the expression goes, "you have to crack a few eggs to make an omelette." So I had to go.

My dad contacted his friends and other family members to get their opinions regarding this issue. It didn't go so well. Many were against this idea. Some even said he would be a fool to send his child to another side of the world because I was so young and innocent. Some people in this world only see the negative side of things without having a little bit of faith that things could turn out to be right. Those people will have hundreds of reasons why something will not work out and almost zero reasons as to why one should do something. That night my dad was devastated and in pain. He told my mother what had happened and what his friends and other family members had said. My mother was a very intelligent and wise woman. She had very strong instincts, almost like a genius. She told my dad these words: "darling, be careful about who you talk your business to because you do not know your friends' hearts nor your family's. Some of your friends will say this out of jealousy and envy not to see your child prosper and have a better living. Believe me, they want you to be the same as them and will say anything for your child not to excel and become somebody. Think about it. Remember, misery loves company."

These words were so powerful to my dad. I believe that changed his mind. A couple of days later, I received the news that I was going to Europe with my mom's younger sister, Jessica. Aunty Jess had a very strong personality that even men were afraid to play games with her or mess around. My dad had so much trust in her based on her character, and he knew she would take good care of me because she feared God and also knew how to behave. I wasn't really excited about going to Europe, as I was just a kid with no knowledge of Europe. All I knew was there were a lot of white people who lived there. In my mind, I thought I would be going there for vacation, but it turned out to be for life without seeing my parents.

I came from a very religious family. My mother always told me never to forget God and to always trust in him, as he's our only faithful friend. She also told me to remember to be wise in everything I do, even when having fun. I kept those words close to heart and gave respect to everyone I met. Being separated from my family was really tough for me, but it had to be done because it was for the best. Sometimes in life, we have to do what needs to be done rather than what we love.

Arriving in Europe

I arrived in Europe in November 2000. It was cold! I was living with my family. It was such a good feeling to see them after a few years, but I couldn't speak a word of English and couldn't understand a thing. I was later enrolled in a primary school. As a child, I was happy to go to school to learn English and make new friends. During those times, late 2000s, it was rare to see a black person walking across Swansea, South Wales. The town was known for racism, and anything could happen. Honestly, children don't tend to think of racism. They just want to be friends with other kids and fit in. Even though I experienced a little bit of racism, it wasn't that bad in the sense of getting physical or dangerous. I believe humans are all born equals. It's just our surroundings and our upbringings that makes us who we are and create the differences. In that school, some kids looked at me as if I were painted brown. They were amazed I was black. To me, that didn't matter. After all, all I cared about was learning the language and fitting in with the rest of my class, who could already speak English and make some friends. In fact, my English still isn't perfect, but that's not the point.

After finishing primary school, I started secondary school where interesting things started to happen. In this school, majority of students were white. It was pretty much a "white school." Did I experience racism in school? Well, a little, but it wasn't that bad. I was in control. Whenever they were name-calling, there was always show time, or shall I say fighting time to be precise after school. It would often be me versus the first bully. Three weeks later, me versus his follower. I was always getting into fights as a kid, but I also kept my position for a long time. I never lost a fight. That was the only way I gained respect. On the other hand, there were plenty of girls at my school who wanted to be my friend. Because I was black, I was different in their eyes. They often wanted to hang out with me and play with my "afro". To them, I was cool. They must have been listening to a lot of Usher or Snoop Dogg. I would often find girls three years older than me in school giving me hints, signals, I mean anything just to hang out with them after school or miss out on class. To them, because I was black, I was the real deal. They figured me out way before I did! So they got friendly and became close to me, but I didn't know what to do at that time. I was an innocent little kid who just wanted to learn.

The other boys called me names just because of the colour of my skin. Boys can sometimes be immature like that. There were rarely any fist fights because everyone knew I could fight because I came from Africa. To them, I was fighting lions and tigers before moving to the UK—how funny! Every time I was called names, I used to go and accuse these kids to schoolteachers. They didn't take it further. All they told me was, "Romeo, c'mon. Are you sure of what you are saying?" This is how I knew there was something wrong with the system, so I didn't give a fuck anymore, pardon my language. I ended up not caring about the name-calling. I inherited a pretty sound mindset from my parents. People may insult me or call me names, but it wouldn't affect me as long as there's no physical contact involved. One of the reasons why the education system keeps failing is because teachers often forget to show empathy towards children. Their main focus is to get them to pass the school curriculum and focus on the upcoming generation, which to me isn't learning. Learning should be fun and interactive. Not I talk; you listen.

All these kids had lots of mouths, but less physical strength. They would call me names in a group, but when I met each one, he'd apologise and run. This is how I knew they were soft. Not only with the name-calling but also from watching how these kids behaved compared to my friends back home. In my country, we were taught to respect all elders, no matter who they were. We respected them because they were older. In my new school, it was the opposite. Everyone was rude towards teachers, and it was the teachers' jobs to respect the children. I asked myself why so many times. I wonder if they were afraid to lose their jobs or be taken to court for child abuse. I found it a bit weird how a child could tell an adult to shut up in front of everyone without getting punished. I was stunned. That's when I realized different places have different values.

The wrong thing I kept doing as a child was the fact that I kept hanging out with these name-calling kids from school, who never liked me because of the colour of my skin. But I didn't care; I just wanted to fit in and make friends. One day I was invited to a "friend's" house for a quick video game tournament. This kid was known as the "richest" kid in our year, with the latest gadgets, new phones, big TV, iPods, anything you can think of. Sometimes he would give away stuff for free because he didn't like it anymore or was bored of it. His dad was a businessman, and he was spoiled. There was a time we were all there playing with his video games. After a couple of hours, his mother came into the house. It was a bit weird, as they knew of me without even talking to me or finding out where I lived. But as a child, I didn't pay attention to all that. I just wanted to play video games and enjoy the night.

An hour later, something happened between my "friend" and his mom downstairs. Because my friend was no doubt a spoilt child, he never knew how to control his mouth; all I kept hearing were swear words coming out his mouth. They were both exchanging words, and I was amazed with the fact that a mother and son can be arguing like this. It was horrible watching them two and listening to what was coming out their mouth, so I decided to go home. It was pretty late when I got home that day, my aunt asked me where I was coming from as it was pretty late for a child to be out by themselves and she had already started getting worried. I gave her a cheeky response just to test what it felt like. It was painful. I was given some serious punishment. This made me understand that I and these kids were too different as I got punished for a tiny rude little response and this boy got away with anything that came out his mouth. The only punishment he received was to go to his room.

My experience in secondary school was terrible. I kept getting into trouble, fighting and failing important subjects. I remember one day I got into a fight with guy just a year above and got suspended for it. It was painful getting suspended from school for something I had the right to fight for, but then again school is school when you fight, you're more likely to face the consequences; which for me was exclusion. I took it to the chin. My dad was very furious hearing this news. He was a very logical man and school played a vital part in his life. He never messed around when he was in school and was expecting the same from me. He didn't want to listen to any of my explanation. To him, I was always in the wrong because I was a child. I don't know, but I think it's an African mentality. African parents tend to believe they are somehow "perfect" that what they say is always right and a child is always wrong in their eyes regardless their explanation. They can sometimes be very stubborn. This does not apply to every African parent, but for the majority yes it does.

They somehow think because they have experienced life more than their children, it gives them some sort of credibility to be right all the time. Which is totally wrong! Nobody is always right, we are all humans, not gods. Even presidents are not always right, just look around what is happening around the world. I was trying to explain to him the reason but instead, he kept telling me how that's not a good enough reason to fight, and that I should never fight again. I took that into consideration and decided not to fight unless there's a strong enough reason to.

My love for football

Football had a powerful impact in my life, even though I was going to school, I always wanted to be a footballer like the majority of other kids in the world, if you ask them who they want to be when they grow up. It was my first love that never loved me back. I was talented playing football but the team which I played for didn't give me the opportunity to shine because I was just different. There was a lot of disadvantages in the city I grew up in. Remember that was back in 2003-2004. Because I was the only black kid playing football for a good club, I pivoted this disadvantage to an advantage. Whenever we had a training session, I would play well to get picked in the starting line-up for Saturday's game. But my Managers couldn't see it, they just never gave me an opportunity to enhance my skills. I would always come as a substitute and to be honest, I hated it. I wanted to play the full game. I met a friend who was also facing a similar problem, he played for a different team. He once told me that in the team he played for, the manager's son was always privileged, he would come late and still get picked, would miss two important games and still get picked the following week. He was always selected regardless of his attendance or game performance. I was surprised to hear that coming from a good player like him. Have you ever been in a situation where you know deep down you're good at something, but the other person doesn't see it or sees it but ignore it on purpose? Yes, that was me and how I felt. For us who had nobody, we had to attend every training session to get picked, and we only got to play in the second half.

Hearing his story and comparing it with mine, at that time, I thought it wasn't fair. Later in life, I understood it's the law of nature. Us as human being we tend to be selfish and only look for what's in it for us. He was also building his child to have a chance to shine in football and one day become a professional footballer. The problem with this team was every time I would come on as a substitute, yet I would always score because I was fast, had quick feet, excellent touch with a good ball control. Whenever I exceeded their expectations, managers and some team players would praise me after the game but all of a sudden, the following week everything will go out the window. I had to prove myself every time that I was good enough to play, so I can get picked. It became tiring. I felt like my managers never took my effort into thought, all they cared about was goal scoring and winning games.

My love for football was contaminated. So in the long run, I just decided to quit my love and give on my passion for football as it was pointless burning off my energy and not getting recognised. Not just with that, but my dad never wanted me to be a footballer as to him footballers were uneducated people with very minimum intellect. He wanted me to be a better version of him. And that was either a politician, a doctor or a lawyer. Football was the last thing in his head. This goes back again to my explanation stating how African parents tend to be closed minded, especially baby boomers. My dad wanted me to go very far with my education, by this I mean going to college, university and graduate and get a high paying job. That was the perfect wish from him to me. Every time I would start a conversation about football, he always tried to deviate from the conversation to a different subject. He would often tell me all the disadvantages of what may happen if I don't turn out to be a footballer and the probability of me becoming one was low. The worse thing about his statements and judgement was he never saw me play. You see what I mean.

He would instead constantly remind me that I could break my leg, or have some sort of injury and then my future will be affected. In my opinion, I believe he was just talking out of fear. The point I am trying to illustrate is, most people only look at the dark side of an event without looking at the bright side. Unfortunately, when you only look at the dark side, you will only see darkness and not light. If he was to encourage me with uplifting words as well as enhancing my dream and give me hope; I would have carried on regardless of what I was facing with my team. I loved football. Who knows maybe I would have switched teams and pursued my passion then. Unfortunately, with all these inputs and being mistreated in the team, I had to leave the team for good and just forget about football.

In the house we lived in, auntie Jess was a mother and a father to me. She played both roles. She took good care of me, sometimes she would even give me a haircut. I love her. She did everything she could, but it wasn't enough for me. Every time she took everyone out for some clothes or shoe shopping, everyone would pick items she could afford, but I would pick the most expensive one just because it looked amazing and felt good trying it on. You see when I was just a kid, I used to love things that shine; I'm talking about good quality of products. I had a good taste from young. Unfortunately, my aunt never bought it as it was too expensive for her to buy. I was mad every time we went out shopping to the point where I never wanted to leave the house because I knew what I was going to get. It took me years to understand her finances, then again, I had to learn to accept what was given to me because bills had to be paid and I wasn't the only child. I avoided going shopping with her all the time she asked and just waited at home for her to bring me what she thought was nice for me, and I had no choice but to like it. After a while, my aunt started noticing that I was no longer interested in going for shopping. She tried her best to understand why and found out. Aunty jess always found ways to make me happy with the little she got. That's when she would then buy me something a little bit more decent hoping I like. I wouldn't say I was a selfish child, I just loved good quality of clothes, kicks, food and even cars.

Problem with the School System

Even though I never liked school, there was only one thing I liked quite well about it, and that was uniform. Because I was such a complicated child, it was easy for me to put on my uniform and just go to school rather than having to plan what to wear the following day. School uniform made my life quite easy. It's more than that, you see in school when you wear uniform it's kind of hard to notice your background, rich or poor. Everyone was treated equally because we were all in uniform. It gives some sort of identity that you belong somewhere, and that you are part of something. Even if you were lost, you would easily be found because of your uniform, it's an identity which I liked. Other than that, I hated the system. When you fail a test in school people often label you "dumb", if you find reading or writing difficult the system will make you believe you are "dyslexic". Unfortunately, many children do believe this, and it does affect their confidence later on in life. This is something I totally disagree with, just because a person failed a test, it does not mean they are "stupid" or have a low level of intelligence. The education system has paralyzed so many dreams and many faiths has been lost. Fear has grown in so many people nowadays that they're afraid to try new things because when they were young, some teacher labelled them "stupid" just because they failed a maths test or for not remembering the capital of Egypt. Well, this book is written to educate you, give you a sense of hope and raise positive emotions for your future and the upcoming generation.

The only time I was happy in school was outside the classroom, my favourite subject was P.E because I just loved playing football and I'm just more of a practical guy. Anything other than P.E was boring. Even P.E became boring when we had to learn some theories. The thing is, I love learning but not the way school teaches. In school they make subject hard for you to understand, it's like their aim is to program you to fail by giving you all these maths equations such as Algebra, Physics, Statistics, Pythagoras theorem, and all other different complexed subject that you will never need in life without teaching us the basic social skills. Don't get me wrong, some of these subjects are very well applicable in different professions but not for most people. Another problem in the education system is that you completely forget about what you learn as soon as you pass your exams. It feels like teachers only want you to get the grade not learn anything out of it, which I found very pointless.

Chapter 2

~Moving to a New City~

4 years later we decided to move to a different city called Birmingham, the second largest city in the United Kingdom. The reason why we moved away from Swansea was that the city had nothing for us. It was hard for a young black African to do well. But, Birmingham was a much bigger city with more job opportunities and a strong community. When moving cities, I decided to take my life serious, abstain from school trouble and do the right thing as I was in my final year of secondary school and needed to pass my final year exams for college. We call it GCSE's. I was enrolled in another secondary school not far from where I lived. This school was the opposite of what I was used to. By this I mean, it was a mixed cultural environment, with a lot of Black and Asian ethnicity and very few to none white English ethnicity. If you came across one white ethnic, they would probably be eastern European. I went from being the only black kid in school to being part of the majority. They were no racism involved whatsoever. It was different. Everyone in this school had some sort of entrepreneurial spirit, you had to find a way to make money in this school. And I liked it. So, I found my own way by selling school dinner tickets and bringing pack lunch to school. I would sell one ticket for £1 and in that week, I would end up having £5 sometimes £7. I would use the same £5 to buy candy and resell it the following week. At the end of the week, I would make at least £12. Then I would use £10 out of the £12 to make more money. The cycle never stopped, I started liking school; I had a lot of customers. Somehow, I found the balance to study and sell in school; I was doing well. The problem with the school system is that they don't

encourage entrepreneurship, they don't teach you how to sell. Learning how to sell is such an important skill to have as a human being. If it wasn't for selling you wouldn't be reading this book. We as human have to learn how to sell in this world of ours. It's a fundamental skill to have. Every time I got caught selling in school, the phone never stopped ringing at home with parent meetings flying left and right. I had to stop my little venture in school and get my grades. This was where I met my good friend Romain. Romain was a good friend in school, he was my very first friend when I moved to this school. We just got along well, in fact we still do. Romain was a similar person to me; we had a lot in common, both in sports, music taste and other outside interest. We just connected. Yet again, because I never liked school, I didn't want to make lots of friends, 1 was enough. I was mainly there just to pass my exams (GCSE) and focus on the future. In school I was a "C" & "D" sometimes an "F" student, I've never got an A. I already knew in my spirit that school wasn't for me as I made a lot of mistakes. I did well in some subjects apart from the most important ones like Maths, English and Science. Doing well for me was getting a C.

College (High School)

I had a lot of trouble with Maths. I was weak in algebra, geometry, shapes, measurements and statistics. I was ok with numbers; simple problem-solving questions. Having to fail my maths at the end of year exam stopped me from studying business studies at the right level like everybody else who finished with me in school. I had to start again at level 2 in college. The school system tends to judge an individual based on paper and not on a factual competitive result. I was studying business studies at level 2, and others who did well in school all entered at level 3 and never sold a dime. I didn't want to start comparing as it wasn't worth it. When attending college, I met a good friend called Maindi, he was a very wise student. He would often finish his work before everyone in class. Everyone knew he would be accepted at university because of his work ethic. To be honest, he was one of the few people who motivated me to do the right thing in college and get the grades. School was everything to Maindi and less important to me because I just never liked the way I was taught. I was glad he never judged me and understood me, we later became friends.

When I would fail a module, he would encourage me not to give up and carry on; take modules seriously and focus on passing. What a good chap.

Throughout my years spent in college (high school) and the launch of Facebook. I got introduced in the world of women. There was a woman who was almost 10 years older than me that fancied me online. She sent me a friend request on Facebook, and we started talking for a long time. She was a kind soul. She was so bold and asked to meet me in person 3 weeks after getting to know her. I was a little bit uncomfortable meeting a stranger, it never happened before and I've never experienced that sort of energy before at that time. So, I refused. She kept persuading me, and sometimes I would avoid her calls on purpose because I knew where it was leading. At that time, I was 17 and she was 26, turning 27, I wasn't interested. One day I just happened to meet her in person in the shopping mall, she made it easy to get along with her. We spoke for quite a while and that was it. I didn't want to start anything with the lady because it wasn't right, the age gap to me was huge with nothing to benefit from; in fact, it could have been someone's wife. The following day I had to tell someone, so I decided to let my friend know about the lady, I told him everything from how I received a friend request to how we bumped into each other at the mall. My friend gave me a good advice, which was to let her go because it could be someone's wife and I knew nothing of her, apart from superficial information. You see, even though this has nothing to do with the school system but somehow it does, I believe the education system should touch on the subject of prudence, self-love and happiness. Our kids spend 6 hours day or more learning about subjects that they may not use their entire life after leaving the education system. Whereas, if we were taught on how to be prudent and avoid certain relationships with self-love and happiness from a young age; we would avoid poor decisions and make good judgements both in partnership and career choices. Our children are not taught this, (if we look closely to one of the reasons why teenage pregnancy is increasing is because teenagers feel lonely, they've never been taught what self-love is, how to make the right choices with partners and parenting. 16-year olds can hardly take care of themselves, yet never mind having a baby. Parents on the other hand, rarely sit down and talk to their children, they tend to leave these responsibilities to the schoolteacher. For this reason, the educational system fails to understand their students). So,

I decided to let her go, the was no future between me and her, it was a complete waste of time. Couple weeks later, as my education life was back on track; there was another girl who came into my life, she was a very nice girl, she was kind, and had a friendly appearance. Well before that time she was. It all started when me and Romain got on the bus coming from town. I saw two beautiful girls sitting at the back of the bus talking. It was a good feeling seeing something attractive.

So, I told Romain to go and sit right beside them so we can hear what these girls were gossiping about. We sat two seats in front of them, suddenly they turned quiet. I was thinking to myself, "what's going on, I'm trying to find an opportunity to get involve in the conversation so I can get to know you and now you two turn quiet, damn!". I decided to play it smart to get their attention. I began to crack jokes with my friend to make them laugh; one of them who somehow was feeling us, started laughing to everything we were saying; that's how I knew she had some sort of interest. I mean, she found me funny, that's rare. I would say something silly on the bus and she would just laugh, you could tell she was waiting to be approached. These were signals which alerted me to move to her, now I was waiting for my friend to get off the bus so I could make the move. Her friend also got off the bus to make it even, that's when I approached. The connection was so strong that she offered to walk me home. I was happy because I met a new friend. This time it was a female friend around my age who understood me. Before entering my house, I asked her if she was willing to come to my church the following day, she was happy and said yes. I was thinking "ok, I got this". She came with her friend to my church the following day, it was a bit weird for her as my church was an African church and she was originally from the Caribbean, but she got used to it. Frankly speaking, she was happy to come because she also met a new friend. We all know how we were when we found a little romance for the first time, she started telling her friends about me and all of a sudden, I was known in her school. She was a popular girl. Almost everyone in her school knew about me and her, it was funny. I used to pick her up after school, sometimes she would leave school early, so she could meet me. When teachers don't show any sort of empathy towards young people, students can get away with a lot of things. And this was one of them. The bad thing about this relationship was the fact that I and her close friends just never got along. It was a shamble, I would try my best to get them involve in certain activities to find a way to know them and get along, but they wouldn't respond to my invitation, maybe they were jealous that I took their friend away from them. It does happen. The poor school system doesn't teach us how to read people. Knowing how to read humans is an exceptional skill to have as it enables you to become aware of our surroundings. Because I was young and inexperienced, I didn't know that their aim was to try everything to break us up. And there was me trying my best to get them to like me as their friend's boyfriend.

We were good friends for a long time until I got accused of cheating by her friends. And She decided to take her friend's side because "they grew up together", "they wouldn't lie to her and would never hurt her feelings". That's what she told me. How naive. I took the blame and had to end the relationship. Couple of days later, I was walking down the road from college and saw her and 2 of her friends coming towards me. Her friends were screaming my name like I was some superstar. I responded back. they were so eager to try and understand why I "cheated" and broke their friend's heart. Can you image? They had a perfect plan to break us up. These were the girls who tried everything to end the relationship. Fellas you see, when your girlfriend's friend doesn't like you, anything you do will always have a negative impact. Even if you save them today, tomorrow they will still dislike you. Its human nature. Unfortunately, I learnt it the hard way. I was in the rush to get into town to buy a gift for a friend who was flying to the U.S. as souvenir. Trying to explain myself to these 2 demons would have been a waste of time. They tried to stop me from entering the bus until I explain what happened as if I was in a court room. I had to get on the bus and got them out the way. They tried to threaten me telling me how they will get me hit by their older brothers because of what I did to them. I wasn't scared.

A month later, it was my birthday so I decided to do a little bit of workout in the morning. That's where I met their older brother at the gym. At first, I didn't know who he was but I felt like something was wrong that day in the gym. My instincts were right. He was twice my height with an intimidating look. Can you imagine this guy offered to fight me on my birthday! How cruel, he didn't care. I was a little scared but at the same time, I didn't want to show him my fear. In school we were never taught how to react in danger, the school system doesn't teach us street smart. By this I mean, how to behave and turn a bad situation in your favour. There are many teachers who know what to say but do not practice what they preach. For example, we have a Physical Education teacher who teaches health but smokes 3 packs of cigarettes a day, we have religious teachers who don't practice their faith, almost an atheist. In addition, we have business teachers who have never run a business or even closed a deal. All these pretenders are killing hopes. I understand it's their profession, but the information passed into our children should correlate with the person teaching. Education is more than just knowledge. In my humble opinion education is being able to transform knowledge into practical and that practical experience need to have some sort of meaning. It has to come to life, not sitting in the classroom.

That day, I didn't want any trouble as it was my birthday. I just didn't want to have a black eye when there are people coming to celebrate with me in the evening. I wanted to look presentable. Luckily, I had Romain with me. Romain was an excellent communicator, he knew how to talk to people and get around their brain. A practical psychologist. The guy from the gym wanted to fight me so bad that I was close to actually giving to him what he was missing. But it was my birthday. Romain had a little conversation with him in the corner to calm him down and explained what happen; then all of a sudden, the matter was resolved. He apologised. By the way, I saw him the other day, he doesn't go around offering people to box, he's humbled now. People skills is another common skill the school system doesn't teach us. We are busy learning and analysing other people's case study without looking in the mirror. This is another reason why it is so hard for graduate to find jobs in their field as they can't even hold a basic practical conversation in the interview process. We are so good talking about other people who found success but never about ourselves. He apologised and moved on. I then called my ex-girlfriend and explained to her what she's getting me into with her friends; she was in tears and told me not to mind them as they are crazy people. We tried working things together from time to time, but it just wasn't working, I had to let go and move on with life.

The girl from library

6 months later, I decided to take my studies seriously and focus fully. If you have noticed, every time I tried to focus, there was always some sort of distraction. The school system has failed on engagement. Students, especially young adults; tend to go to college or university not for education but for the opposite sex and parties. This truth has been hidden in dark silence. Nowadays its very rare to find a young student going to college or university to learn. They do exist, but it's very rare. Their main motivation is always the opposite sex, parties and alcohol. The education system has a challenge to face in regards to this problem.

One day I met a young African girl who seemed determined and dedicated to do well in life and her education. I was impressed. The thing with me was, I just liked being around very smart people in school or college; people who did their homework on time, never wanted to miss class and wanted to do well in general. Those were the people I liked to be around with because I knew they would help me with my assignments or any homework we got in class as I struggle with pretty much everything. I was impressed to meet her and wanted to be her friend. In that college, all pretty girls ever cared about were getting money and having boyfriends. Can you imagine at such a young age? I wonder why students leave college addicted to money and not caring about learning. This one was different she always held her books with her.

So, I approached her and had a little conversation with her. She was genuine, she told me about who she wants to be in the future and how she was planning to get there. I was happy to hear that from her. Later that week I found out by a friend's friend the girl from the library was in an abusive relationship. It could have been an opportunity for me to get to know her at a much deeper level but I just didn't want to do anything with females at this point. You see, opportunities are always dressed in different form. Whenever you hear a complain, it's an opportunity for you to do better. The worse thing about opportunity is that you have to figure it out yourself. Some people have a lot of opportunity screaming their names, but they just fail to recognise it. I also don't blame these people because the school system has never taught us how to capture opportunities and use our instincts correctly. Let me give you an example, I'm writing this book because I've figured out an opportunity that very few people see. I'm not saying this is a virgin idea because we all know that the school system sucks and everyone complains about it. What I'm saying is, I'm able to identify a problem that most people complain about and took action by producing this book that you're reading before most people. I may not be the only one in the market criticizing the education system but taking action and serving the world is what matters. We often go to school learn everything about other people but ourselves. You will often find someone with a Bachelor's degree, MBA or even PhD's but failing to use their instincts in simple day to day common sense activities. It sometimes makes you question their level of intelligence. Not in an insulting way but more in a simple logical way.

The head of Maths

In my final year of college, I did quite well as I became friends with five very bright students. However, I know a friend who failed two of his exams. He was later called into a meeting with a group of his college/high school principals waiting to interrogate him. To be honest, he somehow knew what the call was for and remained calm.

To describe these guys, he would say they all looked angry, suffered from depression and anxiety. One of them was basically threatening him saying it was his last chance having to re-sit a module, failing this module again will result to withdrawing from the curriculum. The education system loves putting fear in students. They want fear to be your primary motivation to do well. Teachers often will use phrases such as "if you don't get to this work done by tomorrow, I will put you in detention for a whole week" or "I will confiscate your phone if I see it again". I'm sure we have all heard something similar to this. The education system believes injecting fear or punishing students will bring the best out of them. In some cases, it does but not for long. When students start being afraid, they often become hypocrites which affect their learning experience. They may tell their teachers they understand a particular subject to avoid conflict or confrontation, but deep down there is zero information absorbing their brain. If fear is our primary motive to achieve greatness in the school system, then we still have a lot to discover about ourselves.

Somehow his threat towards my friend worked, it was almost like a wakeup call to do the right thing. To be honest, he was trying to do what was required, it was just the principal's approach that was poor and intimidating according to him. The worse thing about this scenario was the fact that he had to take a 30-minute test first to be accepted in class. In the college he went to, each student who received D's E's and F's had to take a test to see if they were capable enough to handle the intense course and the pressure that came with it. My friend was worried, he didn't want to fail again. He had seventy-two hours to get his gear on practicing. So, he searched for help from all over the department as needed. Luckily, I managed to introduce him to a wonderful woman called Elizabeth from the college I went to.

Elizabeth was a part-time librarian. She was like a mother to me, she understood most students pain; so, I took advantage of that and introduced my friend to Elizabeth. when I introduced him to Elizabeth, she didn't throw him away with excuses, instead, she was glad we came to her and didn't hesitate to help us because we needed to get accepted into the university. Me on the other hand, I was a D student; I also needed help learning algebra, geometry, fractions and many more. I didn't have to take a test because I got a "high D". So, I was automatically enrolled in the Saturday's class. We had to dive in. Elizabeth was exceptional, she transmitted belief in us. Something the education system fails to do. My friend suddenly had faith, he was confident at this point that he wasn't going to fail this test as he was close to giving up. We spent so much time together preparing for his test in the coming day non-stop. It was tough, but in the end, he managed to take the test in front of two head principals and passed. Thanks to Elizabeth.

The problem with education system is that they don't often guide you. In school or college, there is only one answer any other alternative will be considered as a wrong answer. The librarian (Elizabeth) was not entitled to help my friend as it was not part of her job. She still managed to help him out of kindness, which I appreciate her for. Soon as he passed the test, one of the head said to him "I knew you can do this, you just needed to work hard and you will pass". My friend didn't tell him he asked for help, so to keep it short he said "thank you". You see, what I'm trying to illustrate is that, the school system purely believes in hard work to achieve a certain goal. To me, it's false and simply an old fashion way of thinking. There are many ways you can achieve a certain goal, he didn't exactly work hard; even though hard work was part of it. He just found the right person who gave him guidance to pass the test. If my friend was to take that test without Elizabeth's help, I guarantee he would have failed again. It's finding the right people that count not necessarily hard work.

I made sure I attended every session Saturday morning at 9 am. I had to sacrifice a lot of activities to get my grades. You see, I'm a very ambitious guy in nature but the environment I was in (the education system) was failing me since I found it difficult to adapt to it. The education system does not encourage creativity, we are taught to constantly think like everybody else. Every time I tried to give birth to a new concept, I was told it was not allowed. Hence, we had to stick with the curriculum without adjustments. We were doing what we were told to do, just like in a prison cell. Before the final exam, we were introduced to another teacher called Jannette for extra help. These two women were like angels to us as they provided me and my friend the most help we needed to pass the overall exam. Thank God we managed to pass everything in college and got accepted at the University.

After finishing college, my pockets were so dry- I was broke. I needed to find a way to make money. I was introduced to a guy who was willing to help me find a job. He asked me what kind of job was I looking for, and I told him I didn't mind as long as I was getting money. If you've noticed the response I gave; I was already getting programmed to become an employee, slave for money. Unfortunately, the education system does create employees, money slavery. Those people who often work hard their entire life, could even earn a lot of money but take home little.

I waited for two weeks to receive a phone call from his boss. The day finally arrived, I was called for an interview. The interview lasted ten minutes with a job offer at the spot. That was my first job at the age of nineteen. I thought working was fun until I discovered what I had to do. I was put into a warehouse full of foreigners, they treated them like robots, they didn't respect their existence as human being; to keep it short it wasn't the right environment for me. The worse thing I found out about this place was, most of the workers were educated people with Bachelors and MBA's. It didn't make sense to me at all. I started questioning myself, thinking:

"I worked so hard in college and finally got a place at university and this is what I am seeing?" something is definitely wrong.

I began to question them in a friendly way to get to know them a little and find out how come they ended here and not in the office or in a respectable environment with an MBA. I mean that's what you would expect a graduate with an MBA. It was a sad experience hearing from them. But I later learned something that day. I learned that a degree is not enough to be successful in life. Yet in school, they teach us that a degree is enough to get a decent job. Even with a decent job, a degree is still not enough! The job was way too much for me; I would stand for twelve hours and only be entitled for forty-five mins break. I didn't want to die; I wasn't going to kill myself over chicken change. For some people whom we started with, they absolutely loved this job; to them it was precious because they were getting paid. They didn't care how many hours they worked, as long as there was money coming in. That's when I realised that I was in the wrong crowed, I had to escape. So, I ended up quitting after just three weeks.

Chapter 3

~University~

I was excited to start university, it was a different chapter in my life that I was looking forward to. If I'm honest, I just wanted to get over and done with it as soon as possible. 3 years was a long time to wait, but it happened fast. The first 3 weeks, it felt like university, a lot people, new friends, parties in the evenings, friendly lectures; it was fun. Until I realised it was the same system I've been running from. The system that fears change, the system where you're told what to do without having to question, a system where you learn nothing about money, a system where an average person has no idea what assets and liabilities are, in fact a poison system altogether. It was hard to adapt. You see, we live in a world where change is happening fast, and it seems like the school system is behind with the same old traditional way of teaching. The old tradition of seating down in class and getting lectured, making questions difficult for students to pass, making someone feel stupid when failing without encouraging them to fail, so they can learn from their mistake and do better. We were expected to be perfect at university, even when questioning lecturers. Your question had to make sense to the subject being taught, otherwise, you were looked down upon, even though no one said a thing but somehow you felt little. It was an environment where it was hard to flourish.

My first year of university was easy, I didn't learn anything yet I passed everything. I'm saying easy not because the system made it easy, it was easy because there was nothing added to my knowledge repertoire; everything taught in college I found it at the university. Again, I was in debt worth thousands of pounds over something I did in college. I started questioning myself towards the end of the semester with questions such as "how can I be in debt worth thousands of pounds over something I was taught in college (high school) for FREE?" "how could I have been so naïve and follow this path?" "why are people not noticing this and busy partying?". We were given assignments that could have been completed in less than a week or two, but it took us 4 to 5 weeks to complete a piece of work. Everything got prolonged when it could have been shortened. We would often have 4 hours lecture which I found pointless as everything at this stage was taught in college. Can you imagine in a space of four months we were only given two to three easy pieces of work to complete? To me, this system is something to be reviewed on. I told a friend I was going to quit as it seemed like a total scam and a waste of time. He suggested that I give it time that maybe in the following year it will be different. I thought perhaps he's right, let's give it another year maybe i will learn something new and not just focusing on case studies after case studies. I didn't quit this time.

Second year

It was now the second year of my university experience; this year was challenging, but it wasn't the challenge I was looking for. We kept analyzing different companies, looking at their strengths and weakness with nothing for us. If you've noticed, it's always been about other big corporations and nothing for us as students. By this I mean, helping us rising above situations and becoming better people with simple guidance. Yet, we are getting into massive debts over information that will expire the following day as soon as we graduate. We were slowly getting programmed becoming employees. I want to highlight something important, there is nothing wrong about being an employee. The point I'm making is that the university system has failed to innovate. Nothing seems exciting about university anymore, students learn nothing about themselves but big companies. In the early days, university was the place where people found hope for their future, now university is seen as a place to party, a place where information is out of date the moment you finish the academic year. Something has to be done about the education system.

There was a module on leadership, the irony about this subject was; the lecturer was always late. Can you imagine teaching such an important subject with poor time management skills and expecting people to pay attention? It's ridiculous. I was thinking to myself how can you teach leadership and not be an example words that's coming out your mouth. He was constantly arriving late yet again was teaching how a good leader should behave. There was no excitement in his teaching, maybe because he taught the same module over and over again for over ten years.

I asked him this once, "Sir *you're teaching leadership but why are you always late in majority of your seminars; I mean, most of us arrive on time before you; shouldn't it be the other way around?*" This was his response "*my private life has nothing to do with my profession, I'm here to teach you guys and follow the criteria for you to pass the module, so please do not judge me and let's focus on what's importan*t." I was shocked! I told him we weren't here to make any judgement, the point I was trying to make is for him to be more practical in regards to what he is teaching, not just to follow the curriculum.

The lecturer didn't have any sort of integrity whatsoever but yet he was teaching us one of the most respected subjects of all time- leadership. You see, the problem with the system is that they focus solely on your profession and not you as the person. Whereas, the real world focuses on you the individual and very less your profession. Let me give you an example, you see the moment you leave your working environment, you can be a lecturer, boss, student, mother, father, priest, janitor whatever role you play; the moment you step out the zone which you operate, you no longer hold the role you play from an institute; you basically become a nobody (of course unless you're famous and everybody knows who you are). But for the majority of us, we no longer hold the image or the role we play in society. This means your character plays the role in the real world, not an image or the role you play in society. Unfortunately, the educational system does not acknowledge this fact. To the education system your profession is much more important than your character. My leadership lecturer to me was a liar even though he may have been a good person. The fact that he kept contradicting his teaching, it didn't make sense to me. I was looking at his character, and he was defending his profession; two different worlds.

Towards the end of the first semester, we were given an assignment to pretend to be business owners and design a marketing plan for our potential business and how we were going to run it. It was a good experience, but If you have noticed, I used the word "pretend"; meaning it was not real. You see, the real world doesn't reward pretenders; the real-world reward real players, practitioners not pretenders. We were in the classroom running imaginary businesses while the world was still moving ahead. I felt like I was in a box suffocating.

The education system has failed and keeps failing in this way. The point I'm trying to illustrate here is that business plans are useless, they're just ideas on paper. Business plans only become plans when they are executed; many people fail to understand this concept. If you interview a successful entrepreneur, they will often tell you they had the intention of selling product A, but somehow product B worked. You see, it's the market that steers the actual business; not the 50 slides business plan I did at university. The problem with the education system is that they rely so much on theory without any sort of practical work. Most knowledge taught in the school system is theory based not practical. We spend an enormous amount of time learning about other people's opinions not facts. However, this does not mean everything about the education system is wrong; there are some elements that are still relevant and applicable within the society but overall the system is failing us; we need to do something.

I have a female friend I met at the hub called Vanessa. Vanessa is a very talented student; she has good listening skills with a very charming personality. Vanessa could pick up information without words being passed around- a genius purely by instincts. Her dream was to be a dancer. However, she was facing some difficulty with her career choice. Her parents had put so much pressure on her to go to university and become a Science teacher. She hated every minute of it and was always questioning life. She couldn't understand why she wasn't allowed to pursue her passion but instead please her parents. This is a major problem we are facing nowadays, parents are always pressuring their children to do what they "think" is right for them, without giving their children any sort of alternative. Parents are still forcing their children to embrace a career they have zero interest in, just to make more money.

The system is failing to understand that there are other alternatives beyond university. There is a false prophesy the system is currently advertising. Most universities are subconsciously advertising a message stating you're considered as a failure if you don't attend university- a big lie! Such strong and powerful messages is influencing and dominating at the same time making our parents to send their kids to university, get into huge debt and end up unemployed or doing a job they hate. There's no happiness in that tunnel; especially if you're doing something you hate. Bill Gates founder of Microsoft; Steve Jobs founder of Apple, Mark Zuckerberg founder of Facebook, Henry Ford, founder of Ford Cars, Richard Branson founder of Virgin never graduated from university. Yet their work has changed the world dramatically with such strong evidence that belts the world.

The current education system seems to brainwash a lot of people with the old traditional learning of sitting quietly when the teacher speaks and memorizing their subject at home. Students are totally absent to the current world affairs. They are glued to only their subject whether Science, Maths, History or English. For this reason, they find it difficult to put their technical knowledge in use because they have never been taught how. They consume 90% knowledge and 10% practise. Unfortunately, the real world is the opposite. My advice to her was to do what she thought was right for her own future. If she wants to be a dancer she should chase her dream and find a balance with her studies.

Chapter 4

~Second Phase of Experience at University~

The second semester started, I was happy. I was excited because I was half way towards the end of study. In this semester we were given a module called "career preparation". Everyone was interested as the module was stimulating talk about the future. A lot of hands were up with students sharing their career paths. Some students said they were going into accounting, marketing, human resource was also mentioned as well as administration. Unfortunately, they were no guidance from lecturers or any sort of support after that 45 mins session. In other words, there were no real career preparation involved; students did all the talking. For me I didn't know what I wanted, so I was listening t; it was quite entertaining. I remember that night, I went back home thinking, I never slept. I had hundreds of questions bothering me; questions such as *"everybody knows what they want, what about me?" "I'm I even doing the right course?" "how long does it take to figure out what you want?" "everyone has some sort of security, what about me?"* all these questions were going through my head. I had to look at myself, not in the mirror this time but my inner self.

The next morning came, still no answers, it was worrying. I didn't let it affect me though so I went to my lecture. Most students started applying for what we call a "sandwich year placement". For those who aren't familiar, within the United Kingdom, every student is given an opportunity to undertake a sandwich year where they exercise their skills and knowledge within an industry of their choice. It's part of the course but it's not compulsory. Everyone was busy applying for a job position and started tailoring their CV. For me, I was watching how they went about to do it. Since I didn't know what I wanted and didn't learn anything new, I didn't apply for any position as I had nothing to offer and the idea of being an employee wasn't attractive. I wasn't doing much in that module and suddenly caught a friend's attention.

He came over and asked me *"have you thought about what company to apply for Mr. Olivier?"* … I replied *"No, I don't really fancy taking a year out, I just want to get over and done with university"*. He got curious and said *"don't you want to be secured after uni though; so that when you finish university, you can straight away work for the company of your choice"*. He carried on with his talk *"If I was you, I would start applying before you miss out as everyone is applying, you should take this opportunity"*. I looked at him and said *"maybe I'm travelling a different direction than most of you guys, I don't fancy this. It's not a dream"*. What I'm showing here is that, the education system has indoctrinated us to believe that job security is the most important aspect out of life. We were raised to believe that having a job would be everything without knowing that a job can disappear at any moment. A job is a slow lane to financial freedom, and job income is highly taxed, most employees work harder and live below their means. It's a hidden truth that the education system doesn't reveal. Instead we are accepting what the education system is proposing without carefully analysing. It is time we set people free.

Third year

Final year of university was finally here. This year was different because it went fast. Somehow, I happen to learn something, something completely the opposite of what was being taught. Everyone was learning, doing case studies analysis and focusing on their final year exams and of course; their next career paths. I learnt something different, something they don't teach in the curriculum. Something very important but yet ignored at the same time in the education system. That crucial lesson is called determination. The education system has failed in this lesson. We are not taught how to be determined and pursue what you want out of life or what needs to be done instead. If you remember, I told you I wanted to quit university in my first year; looking back in my third year, I realised that determination played a very important role in me. While other students were getting busy applying for jobs, I started learning about the mysteries of life. It was a good lesson that only happen to appear in my third year. I wondered why just my third year and not first or second. So, I kept it to myself.

As you know or about to know; the last year of university is a very busy year for every student. We are given assignments and exams alongside. So, you really had to balance everything right if you were to finish and get yourself a degree. At this point, I had to turn my horsepower on and do what needed to be done to graduate. I had to study 10 times more than an average student simply because university was not for me and I didn't like it. I tried not to miss out a lecture regardless the weather condition. If I missed any lecture; I'd have to start again at zero. At this point, whenever I lost the motivation, my best friend determination came into my rescue.

Dissertation

Depending on the course you've studied, every final year student is obligated to write a dissertation on a topic of their interest (for some course dissertation does not apply), I was worried. Not because of the idea of writing a dissertation but because I never liked university and nothing was of interest to me. I had no idea what to write about; never mind producing ten thousand words. It kind of funny how I can write pages after pages on this book and had zero words for my dissertation. I was given a supervisor (like everybody else), to shadow my project. Each supervisor had six students to supervise their work performance. In our first initial meeting, she went on to explain how our topic needs to be divided into different sections and what each section would include. She went on and said *"at this point you should be thinking about your projects now, something out of your own interest as having to pick something you're not interested in could potentially lead to failure and lack of motivation."* That was the highlight of the initial meeting.

I was a weak student because I never liked university, I decided to see her. I told her, I had no idea what to write about, I spent the whole year without learning anything about the university. All I kept doing was focusing on passing assignment without actually learning a thing. She took my request into thought and told me to arrange a meeting with her the following week. That night, I started thinking about what to write. I went on to research every single work I had done throughout years spent at university to find an interesting topic. I didn't sleep that night. The next morning came, I managed to find two topics. One was *"The impact of service quality and customer satisfaction in retailing"* and the other one was *"Investigating the impact of online shopping and analysing consumer behaviour"*. Those were the two topics I managed to find. I later picked, the second one just because it sounded better without knowing I would later become an online seller. Life really is full of surprises.

While I was researching which topic to write on my dissertation, I picked up another lesson they don't teach us in school, and that lesson was discernment - making the right choices with good judgement attribute. I had to go through so many ideas to come up with these top two topics. The education system has failed to teach us and is still failing to teach how to make good choices and use discernment. We are being bombarded with plenty of irrelevant teaching that has very little value in today's society. We have many students who cannot tell the difference between good advice and bad advice. To most students, any advice that sound good is good advice because they've never been taught how to practice discernment. They will buy in without careful analysis.

I went ahead the following week and presented her my ideas as well as how I wanted to go about and work. Again, she didn't agree with everything I said as I had to follow the academic guideline to fit the criteria. They were many agreements to disagreements involved but, in the end, we managed to make some adjustments and got on with it. To be honest, at this point I was already tired of university so anything she asked me to do I would do it just to get it out of the way. When I handed in my piece of work, my plagiarism score was high. There is a software called Turnitin, and every student is familiar with this. What this software does is to detect any sort of similarity with existing sources. Since most of my work were from existing sources, I was penalized. I had to rewrite most of the work; it was a painful experience. Thankfully I managed to overcome it and passed.

You see, since we are taught from young to do what we're told; when you step outside the boundaries, we're accused of cheating or doing wrong. Even though my plagiarism score was high it was referenced from various sources, so to me it's not cheating. To me, it's simply using another person's work and implementing it into mine with some element of uniqueness and differentiation with reference. The point I'm trying to make is that we learn from people. Having to write this book took some sort of inspiration from different sources. I didn't just wake up and decide to write a book, it doesn't work like that. There's an old saying by Picasso that says *"good artist COPY; great artist STEAL"*. There's a lot of truth into that sentence. This does NOT mean you should go out and steal. It just means you can take an idea from someone and modify it to make it your own. If we analyze the way the world is evolving; people are simply copying other people's ideas and improving it for the market.

Let me explain with a clear example, the taxi industry has been existing for decades, Uber came and made some changes now Uber is worth billions. Years ago, if I was to tell you that your family member or yourself would be in a stranger's car; you'd think I'm going crazy right? But guess what, it's happening with Uber. Same with Apple; laptop has been around for many years; then apple came and made some adjustment by removing viruses and boom; business exploded. Apple didn't think of reinventing the wheel they took an existing product. People have been drinking coffee for centuries. Starbucks took the same product added a friendly style into it with some uniqueness and boomed, the business skyrocketed. Now we even have a lot of young people drinking coffee because Starbucks made it cool. whereas, years ago coffee was known for old people. They didn't get accused of cheating! People have been watching and going to the movies for years, Netflix simply caught a trend and realised that most people are lazy and would prefer watching series at home; for that reason, they introduced streaming media. This idea alone expanded their business internationally with millions of users worldwide. Sometimes it can be simple. The are many examples I can go on to illustrate; the point I'm trying to make is that the education system is failing to understand that what we learn should be made easy to understand, we should stop searching for virgin ideas, perfect new ideas because there's nothing new under the earth. In fact, it's has been scientifically proven that when things are easy, you learn quick and adapt quicker.

The current education system leads with pain instead of reward. We are given tests and are forced to sit in classes we don't care about with all the fun taken off the subject and, in the end, we're given an exam and if you fail you're looked down upon, sometimes even labelled a failure, low level of intelligence or negligent. The problem with this is we are taught and tested the same material at the same speed of learning without acknowledging that each student learns in different ways and captures information in different methods. Some students are audio learners, some are visual learners, and others are kinaesthetic learners. The way student X learn and captures information will be different to student Y. Unfortunately, the education system does not respect the basic fact of being human, and that each of us are different with different ways of absorbing information. Students who do not learn quickly enough into the school curriculum and fail an exam, often feel low which sometimes affect their self-esteem to even contributes to lessons or talk to their parents about their current educational experience. There is no surprise depression is hitting the roof.

If students were led with reward rather than pain, a lot of changes such as engagement, true interest and execution would take place in the system. Many students will still have the same interest in their course or career after graduating. Unfortunately, that's not the case, as soon as most people graduate, they end up doing something completely different to what they've studied. Just a quick example, If I was to drive an exotic car and a student stops me to ask how I got that car, and I simply tell him that I went to university and read a lot of books to get this car; he's more likely to do well in school because I've shown him what he could get out of school-reward. But that's not the case in school, college or university.

Effective communication

Effective communication was the last piece of the module we had to study before divorcing the system. I spent an entire semester describing and listening to a lecturer teach. There was no practical activity such as role plays scenarios or teamwork exercises; nothing to say the least. Honestly it was embarrassing. Remember there is nothing wrong with description; the only problem with this module was the fact that we spent three to four weeks learning a concept that could have been picked up in a couple of minutes if not half an hour. Do you see why I disliked the education system and why it keeps failing students? How can you take a month to describe something? This concept just didn't make sense to me, I found it very boring and slow. The model below explains the process of learning designed by Edgar Dale in 1969.

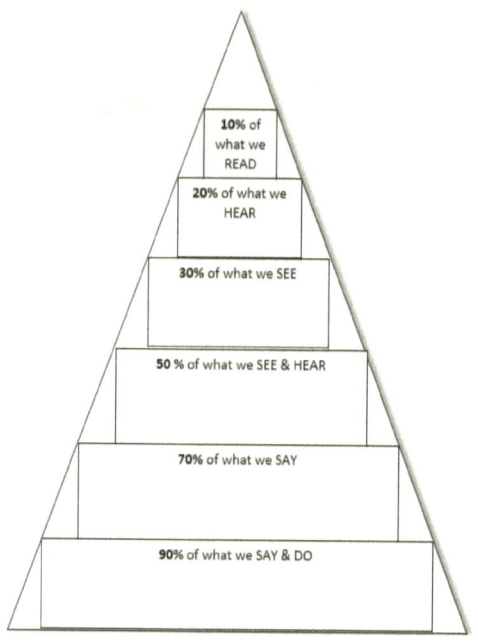

Source: Cone of learning adopted from E. Dale (1969)

The model explains that the worse way of learning is by reading and listening. This alone clarifies why I had a problem with the education system in the first place. Usually, you can pick up a lot of skills in 4 months (semester), in fact I learnt how to drive my car in less than a month. What was so hard about this module? I really don't know. In this class it felt like I was in church waiting for Christ's return. Then towards the end of the term, we had to discuss how effective communication skills has helped us solve our problem throughout the semester and how we were going to use it in the working environment. I was thinking to myself is this lecturer taking the piss? Is he going insane? what did we learn? We spent the entire semester describing words, looking at pictures and following instructions with no new knowledge gained. In fact, it reminded me of college! The point I'm making here is the system doesn't teach us how to accelerate information. After all, it didn't go so well as the majority of the class failed.

Chapter 5

~Graduation~

Seven months later, November 2015 I graduated. It was the day I was finally out of the education system, the day I made my parents proud. Everyone in my family was happy with many "congratulations" on the night. Even though I was somehow happy to be out of the education system; deep inside me, I wasn't happy at all. I couldn't find a job; in fact, this applied with most students. No one was qualified to get a job after university. Those who did find employment, would start at the very bottom; even the A-star students graduating with first class honours. I was shocked. If I'm truly honest with you; that day if you were to conduct an interview and ask each student what they learnt throughout the three years spent at university and how it will benefit them in the market place? I very much doubt they will have a say or even a paragraph to write, especially the business faculty. I learnt nothing about business at university, the only subject I learnt throughout the three years spent was determination and discernment. They don't teach that in the education system. Many people say or have said *"you go to university to find better jobs and a better plan for the future"*. You hear this lie society being said to us all the time. Unfortunately, I bought a lie the society sold just to make family proud, I was naïve.

Employment

I spent months applying for jobs with no response whatsoever. History was repeating itself with what I saw before starting my university education.

There were graduates with MBA working in a warehouse and being treated like robots. I saw it coming. One day I got a call back from a company inviting me for a job interview. I remember my interview very well; it went like this:

Business Owner: "Hi, Mr. Olivier; thanks for applying for this position, tell me a little bit about you?"
Me: "I'm Romeo Olivier; University graduate; in my module, I studied marketing research, consumer behaviour and many more".
Business Owner: "Stop that! Mr. Olivier; Tell me about you"
Me: *confused* "That is about me and what I studied"
Business owner: "Tell me about you as a person"
Me: "oh, I do apologise, let's start again; my name is Romeo; I'm a very determined person; fuelled with ambition, a person who is willing to sacrifice a lot of things to obtain success".
Business owner: "Now we're talking, I'm impressed you understood me, most graduates don't. Now tell me, why did you apply for this position and why would I pick you as my employee?"
Me: *I was very stuck in this question* "Well, I have a lot of knowledge in this field, I love marketing and I'm willing to learn and improve my skill"
Business owner: "Do you have any experience?"
Me: "No, I just finished university and I'm looking forward to learn and grow in your company"
That was a very bad response, I didn't know at the time
Business owner: "let me give you an example; let's pretend you're in the army which one would you pick, someone who knows how to fire a gun and kill the enemy or someone who knows everything about guns but never seen one or used one, which one would you pick?"
Me: "That's pretty easy, I would pick the person who can fire a gun to kill the enemy"
Business owner: "exactly, do you recognize the pattern now sunshine?"
Me: "Oh, I understand"

That was the end of the interview, I never heard from him again. The system has failed us to understand that business owners rarely admire academic credentials, they look for experience. This means you have to think in terms of what you can bring that they do not have, it needs to be something valuable that they cannot afford to resist. In this case, a degree is less important. I still didn't learn. So, I picked myself up and closed that chapter.

Two weeks later, I received a call from GOOGLE, yes, GOOGLE! It was a random and very rare phone call. They called me and said, they really liked my Curriculum Vitae (CV) especially the fact that I was bilingual; it really stood up to them hence they were interested in offering me a job opportunity. Immediately, I said yes! It's google, who wouldn't want to work for them? We scheduled an appointment the following day. When they called me, I felt like I was half way towards my dream, I was so excited. At this point, logic went out the window I just wanted to work for google. The interview lasted forty-five minutes, but it felt like five minutes because I liked everything about it. The following day, Google called me to announce that I was accepted for the job and should start packing my bags; they've got a hotel booked for me in London. I was over the moon; I told my family and some close friends, it was a great feeling.

It was finally my first day at work after graduation as a Field Researcher for google maps launch in the London office. That morning I made a little prayer hoping to have a good day and not jeopardise this opportunity. Everything was well presented, towards the end of the day I was given some work equipment's to have a little play with since they were essentials for my job. For some reason, the devices given to me from work were too complicated for my understanding, I very much struggled with it. Friday morning, I received a call from my manager telling me I was fired. I was in so much shock! I said "why?" She said I was too slow to adapt with tools and they just haven't got enough time to be training people and expected me to already have the skills set before the job. To keep it short; I couldn't solve problem with I.T. I was hurt; I've just started a new job Monday and got fired Friday! It was hard to believe such good opportunity vanish from me. On the same day I asked for a meeting, they refused and told me to look for another job. I felt humiliated. Can you imagine, I already told everyone I found a good job only for them to find out I got fired within a week! What a shame. I picked myself up and carried on with life.

The school system disconnects us from the world's powerful creation of tool, which we need to achieve our dream. We are stuck learning geometry, history, art, geography and other less important subject that can be easily accessible via google, whereas getting taught the practical skillset such as how to start a business or becoming more valuable for a particular position, would have given us huge advantage in the modern world. I was incapable to seize the opportunity as I lacked employable skills; the unforgivable "real world" didn't offer me a second chance. I didn't give up though. I still didn't learn from my mistake and kept applying for jobs. Like Albert Einstein said *"the definition of insanity is doing the same thing over and over and expecting different results"*. That was what I was doing, I was still inside the box and couldn't figure out what was wrong.

The second job opportunity came up. This time I was working as an app developer assistant, at my university. Everything started off well, and as an ex-student I knew quite a few lecturers and we got along well. I pretty much knew what I was doing and my way around. Somehow, I just never got along with my supervisor; I really didn't know why. We just never got along. Two weeks later I was called into the board room regarding my work performance, I was surprised as I completed my tasks on time and things really did go down smooth, but the relationship between I and my supervisor wasn't connecting. After that, I got fired the following month! For the second time! The funny thing about this scenario is that I actually went to this university, which I got in massive debt to study and only to be thrown out of the building. I tried making an appeal and consulting other lecturers to have some sort of help because they were in a better position to influence the decision made. They ignored my emails, calls and completely forgot I was one of their students, all that went outside the window.

I started learning a cruel lesson and carried on with life. This example showed you that the education system will only help you when it benefits them, they want you to apply to their university or colleges; learn nothing and get out with nothing but massive debt with no employment support whatsoever. Don't get me wrong, there are some employment support centres where students have the opportunity to update their CV's, but those are very minimal in comparison to the debt most students leave the university with. Let me explain, if they are a hundred students in the lecture room that want their CV's to be reviewed with only two lecturers, how long do you think it will take them to check each one? Nothing is done properly in the education system hence our students fail to acquire the right skills we need when we meet the "real world". It will be nice to have a refund policy for every university; especially for those students who cannot find employment after graduating. This will be helpful and will benefit a huge number of students like me as university and colleges doesn't benefit most people. I'm not saying that university is a scam and people shouldn't apply to further their education as it does work for some people. People such as doctors, dentists, lawyers, chefs, pilots, plumbers, electricians, mechanics, nurses; university is important for them but not for people like me- entrepreneurs.

When I lost my job, my degree didn't help me; in fact, it was under the bed. It didn't mean anything in the job market, it didn't add any value. The education system does not tell us this; we have to figure it out for ourselves, if you haven't been to university, you're lucky to read this book. Colleges and universities are bombarding us with billboard advertising and controlling us to enter thousands of debts worth of lies about the value of the education by persuading us to go to university. Most students like me don't really know what they're getting themselves into. The worse thing about this scenario is that the government doesn't even ask if the applicant has a job to pay the college or university tuition loan back. We are easily given thousands of pounds worth of loan without any credit check requirement. There got to be some sort of conspiracy behind this. The government could be working on keeping the majority of people poor or in debt their entire life; it's a bubble. We all know the chances of getting a good job is very minimum yet again the government is lending out large amount of money to eighteen-year-olds without questioning.

At university many students assume they will find a way to pay the student loan back as soon as they graduate and find a job in their field of interest. But in reality, it doesn't work like that anymore. The job market is highly competitive with a lot of pressure now and a degree is not enough. It's not an automatic ticket to a bright and abundant future anymore. People who have been in the system and the upcoming generation will need to think about what they want out of life first without having to follow what society is telling us.

Chapter 6

~Another Job Calls~

My third job opportunity came knocking at my door. Since university trained us to be employees and work for money, I took the job opportunity as an administrator. The job was hell! I had to do so much paperwork, attend meetings and work long hours. It was something I really did not enjoy doing. I kept on doing the same thing everyday without any sort of growth within the working environment. I was just exchanging my time for money with no progression. Three months later I got fired again! This time it wasn't as much of a big deal because I never liked the job and I had gotten use to getting fired. It almost felt like every job I got, I was getting fired. I even got scared and discouraged applying for jobs because I knew what will happen next.

Uncle and nephew talk

My uncle was concern about my job firing recurrence. He asked to see me and discuss the issue, maybe I just don't know how to work as an employee, or I have something internal bothering me. I went ahead to see him. This was what he said *"nephew, you have to work hard in this world, very hard and be capable to hold a job. Listen to everything the managers say; even if you don't like it just do it because it's your job, he is paying you, so you have to do whatever he says otherwise you will be poor and get fired again; this is just an advice from me your uncle"*. Of, course it was an advice, but one advice coming from a person I didn't want to be like in the future. My uncle didn't have financial freedom. Hence, I did not want to listen to his advice. At this moment he was thinking like an employee, and not like an entrepreneur. To me, this sounded like this "your boss owns you, you have to do whatever he says; work long hours if necessary; if the boss don't treat you right deal with it, its life." that's how it came across. What a cruel way of living life! He was ignorant and just couldn't understand my way of thinking. I told him there's a reason why I can't keep a job, I just can't work 9-5. It's not for me. He said *"don't play with yourself son, just work like everybody else"*. Again, he knew nothing about entrepreneurship. So, I didn't buy into that advice and moved on. When I was trying to look for a job even my lecturer didn't help me, but he was the one teaching career preparation. I want this book to reach as many people as possible; do you really think marketing from university will help me do this? I doubt it. In fact, my lecturers don't even know how to sell a pen never mind having to sell a book across the world, but he has a Ph.D in marketing, a "marketing professional." I'm not writing to judge universities or their lecturers. Most lecturers are good people outside of university, it's the educational system that I believe is corrupt.

You see the core of education has to be about discovering your purpose of life and navigating towards your destiny. Education should be like a puzzle that's given to you, and you have to figure out which puzzle makes what to identify who you are truly. I believe we should be taught the following subjects:

- Personal finances
- Public speaking
- Sales
- Creativity
- Persuasion
- Determination
- Patience
- Mental Fortitude
- Problem solving
- Self defence
- Discipline
- Wealth
- Debt

- Health
- Faith
- Courage
- Taxes
- Real Estate
- Love
- Reading (interesting books)
- Happiness
- Simple maths
- Self-esteem and many more meaningful and valuable lessons that will contribute to our lives in helping us become better people, that's where it begins in my opinion.

The current system does not teach us how to pick our career. This is one of the most crucial part of our lives as we spend most of our time in a certain occupation. And most people are working on the job they hate, can you imagine how terrible that feels? Spending 8 hours or more doing something you hate, everyday! I'm not trying to make you feel bad if this applies to you as I've been there myself and I know how it feels. What I'm trying to do is lighten up your spirit and show you that there's another side of the world that most people do not see. There is still hope for a brighter future, but you just have to practise and be in the right direction. The thing is, you know you're in the right career if you're excited to wake up and go to work and time is flowing as your job is effortless, if this sounds like you then congratulations! Your career brings you joy. You don't necessarily look at the clock because your occupation gets you to forget about the world and it feels as if you're not working. I believe it's better making less money doing something you enjoy than more money doing a job you hate as this brings depression, anxiety and stress.

I have a very talented friend, who has the potential of becoming a poet. When she starts reading her poems, it automatically positions you in a different world. It feels so real. The only problem with her is, she doesn't recognize her talent, no one has ever told her she was good. Every time she was to read her poems, family members, school friends and teachers will often tell her that what she's doing is a waste of time, no one would want to listen to her, she should focus on what's important. Now as I'm writing, she works in McDonald's, she's a single mom with three kids; struggling to pay her bills. Life could have been different. I'm not saying there's something wrong working in McDonald's; what I'm explaining here is that the current education system has crushed dreams. We have too many young creative people in the wrong field of work. They have been trained to do what they were told at the very young age forgetting their uniqueness and just following the trend. Time passes, dream dies, unfortunately for many there's nothing but regret when you look at their eyes. This book is here to give you guidance, courage, mental fortitude and the belief that anything is possible regardless of your age. If you have children or planning to have any in the future, please talk to them. Let them do what they want and simply give them direction as well as guidance and support.

A couple of months later, I met an old friend from school who is now a manager for a sales company. He was surprised at how I still couldn't get a job. He suggested to hire me without an interview as we were good friends in school and made a lot of sales back then. I accepted the job. My first month at work was terrible! I was given all these types of script to memorise and jump on the phone for eight hours trying to close a deal. To be honest, it was a good experience, but I wanted to do it for myself, and not for a company. I was putting so much energy for commission pay only, so I felt exploited. I looked on the other side, and I saw the owner of the business relaxed with a drink on his left hand. I was annoyed. There was too much script to memorise and it just didn't feel real. I didn't last long, I fired myself. And That was the last job I had in an office environment.

Chapter 7

~Trip to South Africa~

As you may have noticed, I started blaming everyone but myself. My old self was blaming the job but me. To tell the truth, the real problem wasn't the job, it was me! I couldn't handle it. I just wasn't made for a 9 to 5 working environment like the school system is training everyone else to be. Yet again, I still wasn't learning. Somehow, I wanted money but had zero employment skills. One day I decided to take a trip to Cape Town, South Africa to visit some friends. This holiday was an eye-opener. This is no envy, but my friends lived an extraordinary life. Their comfort was above average, I was astonished. So, I started digging some information asking them what they do and how they lived such a lavished life. They told me what they did, but it still didn't make sense to me at all. The good thing about this holiday experience was the fact that I discovered something different, a different world. The only problem with this world was, it was blurry and didn't make sense to me.

Two weeks later, I got back to England and started doing some research on the internet. It's so amazing how things happen. Sometimes in life, you need a change of environment to open up your eyes and discover the mysteries of life. Three days later, my sisters wanted me to drop them off at the airport; they were flying to Ohio, America. Throughout the journey, I remember researching on google *"the difference between rich people and poor people"*. My God! Things started to appear, I started discovering a different world. The world they do not teach us, the world our parents never taught us, the world the education system doesn't even know it exists; automatically I bought a book. A book by Robert Kiyosaki called

"*Rich Dad Poor Dad*". This book revolutionised my thoughts, brought my spirit back to life and opened the door for curiosity to set in. I became very curious about figuring out the difference between the rich and the poor.

I never read an entire book at university as I found reading daunting with complexed philosophy, but this book (Rich Dad Poor Dad) was not just different but special. If you haven't read it yet, I want you to get a copy. The book thought me a lot of things in a space of three weeks. I learnt the difference between traditional education and non-traditional education, financial literacy, history of taxes, the power of corporations, investments and how to mind your own business. If I'm honest, I never knew non-traditional education existed as the education system never talked about it. In my mind, I thought the word education meant going to school or university to become an employee. That book changed my philosophy of life, as I discovered another way of learning. I was mentally born again.

The education system has made us believe that having a job is everything a person need to have to have a good life without acknowledging that a job is only a short-term solution to a long-term problem. If you observe carefully, you will often see that most people work everyday without having to question if there is another way to create income. They are often satisfied living pay cheque after pay cheque without realising that there's more to life than doing a job you hate. When they are mistreated at work, quitting the job is the very last resort in their mind, they prefer being treated like slaves as they are getting paid for it. Money controls their lives. To me, I wanted to meet Goliath and destroy him, not mask symptoms like living cheque after cheque, and doing something I hate.

If you read Rich Dad Poor Dad, you will understand that money is an illusion that most people chase. Money is an illusion because it's infinite, the more you chase it; the more you will need it with zero satisfaction till death. In fact, the more you chase money, the more you're taxed. Getting taxed is another way of getting penalised for chasing money, and yet again most people still do not grasp this concept. They pursue money their whole life and miss out on life. You see, chasing money is life's biggest trap as it becomes your master, not your servant. The education system has failed and keep failing us to understand this; we are inculcated to believe that money is the master and we should be inferior to it; just like our school teachers. I was fortunate enough to overcome this force because I never had the fear to quit my job as this sound scary to most people.

I have a distant uncle who worked like a slave just to buy a big house and a nice car. Well, he's a friend's uncle, but we call him uncle. He spent twelve hours a day doing a job he hated. Everyday after work he was angry, he will always complain about his house bills with very small or no social life. In addition to this, he would rarely spend time with his wife and kids; things were getting out of hands due to his absence at home. A couple of days later he fainted at his job due to lack of sleep. Now as I'm writing this book, the doctor told him to reduce his hours at work and get some rest. Rejecting the doctor's advice might be calling an early death. He no longer works like he used to, didn't buy the dream house or the car he wanted. This was a glimpse of the future I didn't want to have, hence the idea of having a job since university wasn't attractive, I was surrounded with people who hated their job, yet spent hours doing the same thing they never enjoyed. I was no different than them, hence, I had to create my own path. At this point, my education started. This time it was a different sort of education, it was self-education.

After finishing Rich Dad Poor Dad, I fell in love with what I discovered, and I decided to purchase another book called *"Retire Young Retire Rich"* by Robert Kiyosaki. In this book, I found out the importance of Controlling your own reality, Having the right mindset, Real Estate, Generosity and the Power of words. Those subjects are often hidden from the education system as we are taught very minimum information even at university level. It's appalling. The education system needs to be revisited and teach us more about the principles of life as right now we are fed day by day information on how to mind other people's business, solve their problems and forget about our own problems. After finishing Retire Young Retire Rich, my mindset starting to change. I became a student of wealth.

Chapter 8

~Hunger for More~

I was determined to find my way to success regardless of how long it took. I started reading books after books and studying outliers, people who rise above the masses. It was an interesting journey. While studying these people, I noticed they were very exceptional; they knew exactly what they wanted out of life, they were very adaptable, non-cynical, associated with the right people and had mentors. The education system doesn't teach us how to find good mentors, people who want to give you guidance and help you win the game of life. In school, once you complete a year, you simply move on onto the next without any sort of mentorship. Hence, a lot of students and young people are lost. Since I never had a mentor myself, I found myself in books, my books became my mentor. I was constantly reading and watching videos of the people I admire. I found out that, outliers were very optimistic and were never afraid of the future. I had to adopt this character.

Friends and family

There is one piece of advice I will like to share with you, when you start learning about wealth you should always control your environment, by this I mean your friends and family. When I became a student of wealth, I noticed that I and my friends were becoming very distant. This is not to say in a bad way, or in any form of superiority. I just felt very different to them; it felt like we were traveling opposite direction. The way I began to think and process information was very different to them. Most weekend they wanted to party, I read a book, when they would go on holiday, I would use that money for holiday and buy a course online, many of them will look for a job, I would attend a networking event, others got married with children, I was still single living in a studio apartment learning and discovering the truth for myself. This is a crucial point I'm making because the education system does not teach us anything about choosing our circle of friends.

Many people are conditioned and afraid to change their circle of friends because they don't want to be judged and want to fit in. The problem with this is that when you cannot control your circle; nothing works. Marriage don't work, relationships don't work, business don't work, even your career won't work. We have all heard the saying "you are the average of the five people you spend your time with". The system has never told us anything about this, I wonder why. I was convinced I was in the wrong environment and needed to change my circle of friends. This does not mean I got rid of my friends but it only meant that I had to create space for some new friends with similar interest as myself, people who were curious, hungry to succeed in life and become independent financially. I wanted change in my life. I started joining clubs and online groups of like-minded people.

Unemployment made me rich

Even though I felt rich spiritually and began to think like a rich man, I was still financially poor. There was no evidence of my way of thinking. By this I mean, everything was internal, the world couldn't see it. All the world saw was a young unemployed person. But I saw a giant in me, and I had to do everything to bring it out and show it to the world. I had to prove myself that I could rise above average. My perception was my reality. Some people would often question me in a heated debate "*who do you think you are?*". Some people thought I was a "spy", but I laughed. It's amazing how people treat you when you consider yourself as a minority. I would often reply saying "*I'm just like you, but I think a little bit different*" not to sound intimidating. One advice I kept from my elder was this "*in life you have to think big but always remain humble as we both don't know what a human being is capable of doing*". I made sure I always came across humble with everyone I came in contact with and never showed any sort of pride with the information I was getting, I had to balance things right.

Since I was cash poor, my savings were running low and I needed to raise capital. To be honest with you, even though I felt rich and began to think rich; I still didn't know how to make money. What I knew for sure was, I never wanted to apply for a normal 9-5 job as it wasn't for me. One day I went to see a friend who worked in a retail store and I told him that I needed a job. What I like about this friend is that he was honest. He said *"brother, I don't want you to apply for this job as it doesn't suit you. Even if you did apply, make sure you don't stay here for long; do what you have to do and get out of this place. I'm only working here because I have to feed my son and wife. If it wasn't for them, I wouldn't be here. I'm looking to get out of here"*. I did appreciate his openness. When I applied for this position, I made a lot of sacrifices, I had to put my pride aside; I lived below my standard for quite a while but my destination, perception and commitment never changed. I knew what I wanted and was willing to sacrifice. The education system teaches you 1+1=2, and many people live with that reality. To me that is a very short way of thinking. To me, I saw 1+1= anything you want it to be. I was willing to take such a menial job because I knew one day I will rise. To me it was always about playing the long-term game.

It's more than that, another reason why I applied for such low-level job was not because of money, even though money is important, but it was mainly because I wanted to focus on myself. I had a strong passion to change my life and study the subject of wealth. Hence, I had to reduce the number of hours at a job and mainly focus on my journey. I discovered something else, becoming a student of wealth I found out that the education system rarely teaches us passion. To me, passion is the combination of love and anger. Love because of the person you're going to become in the future and anger because you're not that person yet in the present. Teachers at school or university do not show us how to identify our passion. In the education system, there are no personal subject where children or students are asked to identify their strengths and weakness and really question what they are good at and how they can turn that strong passion that they have to serve the world. The system does not seem to care at all about this crucial point and only want us to become employees obeying rules without questioning. We have graduates chasing high paying job as soon as they graduate without questioning themselves first. They want a high paying job and live a life receiving earned income. Most people I graduated with were heavily focused on their job with very little to no self-discovery. With me it was the opposite, I got a very low-level job and I focused heavily on myself, discovering my purpose. A good job was irrelevant in my case.

My first few days doing retail was painful. I had to stand for eight hours, doing nothing but serving customers. Sometimes I felt like a robot having to repeat myself serving different customers. However, the only good aspect of the job was the flexibility; meaning if I wanted to work, all I had to do was call the manager and he would put me into the system. I had a choice to work or not to work. Besides that, I only worked once or twice a week. The rest of the week was for myself working out the puzzle of life. Did I love the job? Hell No. It was passion that was the fuel to my motivation towards a bright future. Every time I would attend work something weird will happen. A regular customer one day walked in to do her shopping. She saw me and approached me in a very usual way asking for my age. She said *"son how old r u?"* I told her I was 24 (at the time). She carried on *"are you looking for a better job?"* I told her *"No, I'm working here, why would you ask that?"*. She replied *"this job is not for you, why don't you become a plumber or an electrician, don't work in a supermarket. My son is a plumber, you should go to college and study it so you can become a plumber"*. I didn't want to tell her my plans, so I just laughed about it and let it slide.

Two months later, another customer comes in, and while browsing looking for what to buy, I was having a conversation with him. He asked me how long I've worked in the company, I said *"not long"*. He said *"you don't belong here, hurry up and get out of this place, I can honestly say it's not for you"*. I knew the job wasn't for me, but that wasn't the point why I was working there. I had friends and some family members asking me to go back to university and get a Master's degree, maybe I will have a better chance of securing a better job. I simply laughed. You see, everyone's journey is different; what worked for person X will be different to person Y. Instead of feeling sorry for myself and getting angry I used them as motivation to chase my dream.

The road of success or self-discovery requires a lot of patience, mental fortitude as well as mental habits. We have a lot of talented students who lack patience. So many people want instant gratification without giving it time to flourish. This can be in a relationship, friendship, career and in business. When time gets tough, and things don't appear the way it should, the logical thing to do for most people is to quit. Unfortunately, those people miss out a lot of good surprises life has to offer them. We all have heard the saying "winners never quit and quitters never win". There's some truth in it. Mental habit is such an essential factor that the education system ignores. We are not taught how to overcome discouragement, self-doubt, fear or negativity when it sets in. Having a strong mental habit will enable students to rise above negative forces such as bad friends, day to day problems and just shut it down. Instead, in school we are given very limited subject to memorise. Limited in the sense where it can only be applied in one particular field. Information gathered from the education system does not transform into real practical value, besides being good at a single subject. A very outdated way of learning

Financial education

From time to time at work, I would often question my colleague just to see how knowledgeable they are. I would often ask them if they read. Many of them did say they read, but they read local newspapers. I asked again if they read interesting books on financial education. Again, most of them said no, money is not important; they are happy doing what they're doing and are not looking for more money. But these are the first people lining up asking for overtime to pay their bills and play the lottery. I didn't quite understand it at first; It took me sometime to understand what they meant. After a while, I realised that most of them were ignorant and lazy to think for themselves. It was difficult for me to transfer my knowledge to their brain as they've already become products of the environment. There's an old saying that states "you can't teach an old dog new tricks". Even if I tried explaining to them a different way of thinking, they would still go back to their old way of thinking as their chains were too strong to let go of old habits.

A few days later, some of my colleague came to see me and said *"we invest in the company's share, I'm sure that is some sort of financial education?"* based on what I read and what my mentors have told me I replied back by saying *"I'm not an expert in this domain, but all I know is there is no financial education in mutual fund. This is because somebody else is managing your money (the company) and you on the other hand you're not learning anything from it. when the company make a win or a loss based on external or internal market forces you don't gain any sort of experience".* One of them replied back frustrated saying *"of course, its financial education the company is saving money for me and I get a certain percentage increase after a set period of time".* I replied back and said *"you may see it as that and that's totally fine, but what I'm saying is you're not learning anything when you invest in mutual fund, in fact there's nothing mutual about mutual funds; the guys running the funds (company owners) are the guys getting rich not you"* he then said *"what do you suggest we should do at this point then".* I asked *"out of interest how long have you been working here?".* He answered *"fifteen years"* I then said *"I'm not in the position to tell you what you should and shouldn't do, it's up to you. But if I was you I would start with buying a book Rich Dad Poor Dad to begin with as it taught me a lot and revolutionised my way of thinking".* The conversation ended. It's amazing how Rich Dad Poor Dad was launch in 1997, yet most people are not aware of the book today! We should read more.

I later I noticed that evening that the education system has failed to teach us financial education, how to invest, reproduce and create another source of income. I just couldn't believe how someone would work for fifteen years with only one source of income. Most people know how to add and subtract but when there's finance involve there's a handicap in the equation. Most people cannot multiply their investments. To me it wasn't making any sense I had to do some research to understand the why. I purchased another book, called *"Increase Your Financial IQ"* by Robert Kiyosaki. Even though I do not know Robert personally, to me, he became my mentor. He was my guide throughout my financial path. I always went back to his books to gather information before making any financial decision. In his book Increase Your Financial IQ, Robert highlighted *"It's financial education that enables people to process financial information and turn it into knowledge ... and most people don't have the financial education they need to take charge of their lives".* I agree with his statement. The system has isolated this knowledge from us, it took me more than 5 years to finally understand how the world operates; we were programmed by the education system to live a tough life working like slaves and never find the abundance of life.

At my workplace, the manager will often ask me if I wanted more hours of work. I would refuse, he once said *"how can you refuse to work, don't you want money; don't you pay bills at home?"*. I would then reply *"no thanks, I am happy the way I am"*. I knew what the truth was and I was running from being cog into the system, working for money. I wanted freedom, and I had to invest time searching for that freedom, not chase money. Every time they asked me to work more, I would always refuse. One day my boss threatened to sack me from work as I always turned his offer down. I asked him first why he would do something horrible like this? He replied by saying because I keep turning his offers down, now he feels like I'm his boss. I felt sorry for him deep down, I knew he was stuck in a rat race. that's why I replied back to him by saying *"We made an agreement, you put me on a zero-hour contract, and I'm totally happy with that, I don't need to work more or less; what I am doing is totally fine and it suits me"*. he kept applying pressure but I kept refusing. Since I was working on a zero-hour contract, I was focusing more on cultivating skillsets of an upcoming entrepreneur, not an employee.

Chapter 9

~More Lessons of Wealth~

One day I was travelling to London, my manager gave me a call asking me to cover a member of staff who was sick and couldn't attend work. I told him I wasn't aware of it and took a trip to London for a couple of days. For some reason, he wasn't pleased with what I said, so he gave me a warning. I said calmly that I wasn't aware of the emergency cause if I was aware I would have gone to work like everybody instead of travelling, so I then apologized. Frustrated as he was, he hangs up the phone. Instead of panicking like most employees would when their line manager reacts like that; I was calm and enjoyed life, I didn't let his reaction affect me; it didn't matter. When I got back from London the problem was solved, I got back into work. Sometimes it's easy. What I'm showing you here is that many people let their boss dictate their life just because they pay them a few bucks; it wasn't the case for me. Nothing intimidated me at work since I wasn't motivated by fear and getting fired was no big deal. This is not to say I sabotaged the job or I wanted to get fired, of course I didn't. Getting fired didn't scare me as I knew who I was and what my value was worth.

What I noticed at work was that even though I worked much less than most people in the company; everyone struggled financially. I was thinking to myself, shouldn't it be the other way around? I will talk to my colleagues who worked Monday to Friday, and they will <u>simply</u> pour out their financial struggle even though they had a full-time position. The problem with my colleague and most people is that; they believe money is a solution to most of their problems. They will often come and tell me how bad they need money and desperately need a pay raise without acknowledging the fact that financial education solves money problems. Even If they worked overtime, they soon become broke regardless the amount of money. This can be applied with many lottery winners who suddenly go broke after twelve months. One of the reasons why people stay wealthy is because they learn how to solve their financial problems by planning way ahead before the problem gets bigger and use their intelligence to generate cash. Financial intelligence solves money problems not money.

My job wasn't that bad because I had the privilege to question my colleague personal questions to understand their core value and belief. I asked the store manager if she enjoyed her job. she said she loved it. I was thinking to myself wow! Then I asked, *"why?"*. She replied saying *"I like working here because the company takes care of me, it's a pay cheque guarantee at the end of the month, I get holiday pay with many other company benefits"*. There's nothing wrong with this answer, just that to me it did not make sense. We had different views of life and core values. She wanted job security and promotions, whereas I wanted freedom and hated job promotion. We have been spooned fed since school to follow instructions and become consumers not producers. She wanted to be labourer for the rest of her life, and I wanted to be an entrepreneur to later become a capitalist.

Throughout my journey of becoming an entrepreneur, I noticed that the education system has failed to teach us the subject of motivation. This means, what motivate people, their inside emotions and how to overcome stress and procrastination. Procrastination does kill dreams there's no secret in that; it's the truth. Many people procrastinate, they wait six months to acquire a skill that could have been picked up in two weeks. The education system is failing by not focusing and understanding what motivates their students to attend their classes at core level. For example, what motivates me to write this book is to serve the world by providing practical knowledge, correcting an injustice behind the system and live a mark that I've accomplished something concrete with a positive impact as there are millions of people currently facing a lot of problems due to lack of proper education. Another motivating factor is that I never wanted to be somebody's b*tch when it came to money, I never liked the idea of working a 9-5 status quo, I want to travel the world with my future wife and help my family as well as provide for charity and orphans. I promised myself that I would live an elegant life where I don't have to worry about my finances. You should find what motivates you as well. I wish they taught me this in school.

If you have noticed universities and colleges has been misleading the public with false statistic to make them appear important in the eyes of the public. Many universities give random figure of students finding employment after graduating when we both know many students suffer after they finish university. Don't get me wrong some do find success within their field, but the majority of students do not. Universities and colleges spend huge amount of money on construction projects across the UK and other part of the world; renewing libraries, gyms, housing units, and other facilities with the aim of attracting students, introduce them to the world of debt and completely forgetting the actual core concept of education. It's becoming a business. Some universities including the one I went to advertise that more than half of their students find employment after leaving education, what a fat lie. The unfortunate reality is that graduate are only employed by McDonalds, Supermarkets, Warehouses and other low skill level jobs. The education system is manipulating the public, and a lot of people are falling to the trap called fraud.

A day out with a friend's dad

I know someone whose dad is highly educated; his dad holds two Master's degree; in two different subjects. Every time you tell him something, he will usually stop you and say *"yes I know that"*, even if he doesn't know a thing. We often call him "Smarty mouth" because of the way he behaves whenever you communicate with him. The problem with him is that he judges people based on their appearance and suffers from inferiority complex, even though he's educated. We were driving on the motorway once, and two guys in a Bentley drove passed us. He looked at us and said *"you see these guys, they are not cheap guys sons; I can never afford a car like this with the family I have"*. I was thinking to myself what are you trying to say. From my perspective, he was self-prophesising that he would never have a Bentley. That day in the evening, he then asked me what I wanted out of life. I told him I wanted to become an entrepreneur, run a business and achieve financial freedom. He laughed at me saying *"Son, in this world you can never be financially free; there are problems after problems in this life, find a good job and build a family"*. Again, I didn't listen to his advice because I knew it was coming from a poor background, with a poor reality of life. I shut it down.

Even though he is highly educated and holds two Master's degree, to me he's still a guy who hasn't found his purpose yet. He has a menial job with a lot of academic knowledge, there is no correlation to that. This is not to judge, we have a problem in society that need to be solved. A lot of people are facing this problem today because the education system does not give students a roadmap or an indication to success. The system does not focus on our upbringing and does not question what else we learn from outside of school. We come into school learn whatever is taught and leave class without a map. If we look closely and analyze, we will see that many people who found success in their life had some sort of roadmap which they followed. Even when they failed their direction never changed; they were persistent, carried on until success was found. This is a vital point that the education system does not give us. We lack competitive advantage. We have students who just believe that because they come from a certain family they are entitled to success as if the world owes them something. This is a selfish way of thinking because the world does not owe anyone anything. We need to understand this as it's the cause of many heartbreaks. We live in very narcissistic environment, where people automatically think they deserve the best without putting maximum effort. If you have this belief, please bury that thought. Looking over the other side, I strongly believe anything is possible in the world we live in. You can accomplish anything if only you put your minds to it, especially with the help of technology. Technology has given us access to a wide range of information with no borders. We can search for practically anything with the use of the internet and find what we desire. I strongly believe it's the best time to be alive and for entrepreneurs to rise.

It Was Time to Action

As you may recall previously, I knew all these truth about wealth with no evidence of my knowledge. One day I sat down browsing on YouTube, and I found an advert. I usually skip past YouTube adverts because I find them annoying, but this one was different, it caught my attention. It was a young guy about my age talking about how the internet changed his life! He said doing business online made him retire at a very young age and he is willing to help other people do the same. I was thinking to myself "*damn, this is something interesting, I have to take action*". I immediately joined his webinar. In that webinar, he explained step by step how his students were making money using Electronic Commerce (E-commerce). To be precise using Shopify drop shipping and how these results are achievable regardless of your background. This woke me up. I decided to join this venture.

Since I didn't know how to start and where to go, I thought it would be smart to just contact one of his students who lived in Marseille (France) and work with him. That's what I did. I looked up for his name on Facebook and sent him a friend request. Luckily, he accepted me. I was looking to build a bond with him straight away and not come across as weird. When he accepted my request, I first of all started by congratulating him, and stating how impressed I was with his results in internet marketing. I made sure there was a bond before telling him what I wanted. This is one of the tricks I learned in life. Before you want someone to offer you any sort of service, you have to offer them some sort of value first. This could be from buying them a gift, recognition or giving them a simple compliment. Value can be added in absolutely anything, people like to feel important. I was honest with him and told him I wanted to work alongside him fifteen minutes into the conversation and he agreed.

This seemed too good to be true, but I didn't want skepticism to win my thoughts, so I immediately asked for a face to face meeting for reassurance. Again, he agreed to meet me in person because he intended to do business in the English market and was looking for an opportunity to expand; I was happy to hear that. I remember that night I slept like a King, I was getting closer to my goal. I took a flight 3 days later to Marseille to meet him and discuss how we were going to run this venture. I was serious and he could see it in my eyes. There was no service agreement or any sort of signature, my words and the action I took was the recipe of my loyalty. He suggested to include a graphic designer in this adventure, that was it; partnership was formed. We started working and figuring out what niche we were going to create our online presence in with Shopify. After some pros and cons, we finally decided to focus on the baby market.

It took a while to understand the buying behaviour in the English market. According to him, English and French buying behaviours are different. I was just a learner and didn't know much about drop shipping all I did was listen. He showed me everything, from how to turn strangers to customers on the internet. I was amazed with the information I was getting, I first thought social media was a platform to communicate with people and stay in touch with them, but he changed my mind. Social media to me is now a business with millions, if not billions of customers worldwide. It was such a humbling experience. Day after day we were trying and testing the market with different product launch. It wasn't easy. Until one day we identified what was missing and plugged it into the process. In less than three months we managed to accumulate eighty thousand pounds! I was amazed! That's when I knew I was going to win the game of life, and becoming an entrepreneur was by far the best decision I made. I also realised that you become like the people you surround yourself with. It started making sense as I was living it, not just theory. There's a famous quote from Albert Einstein that says *"everyone is a genius, but if you judge a fish by its ability to climb a tree, it will live its whole life believing that it's stupid."* This is very true.

I never liked university and having a job wasn't a dream because a job is limited. Don't get me wrong, I love learning and I'm a very curious individual. The problem is, learning the way the education system is set up was not for me and having a job would automatically stop my creativity, I like to try and test a lot of things. This is why a job or university couldn't bring out my full potential, no matter how hard I tried, I was always told by someone else to follow instructions, anything else would be the wrong thing to do. It just wasn't my environment. Going back to the results I gained doing online marketing (drop shipping); if I'm to be honest with you; it wasn't the amount of money that got me excited. What got me thrilled was simply a different way of thinking. I realized that I could make money using different methods while my friends and most people I knew were doing a job they hated, I was getting ahead financially. It took me three months to make £80,000, as an employee it would have taken me more than 5 years. That's when I discovered another lesson they don't teach us in the education system, that lesson is called Leverage.

Leverage simply means putting in less effort and earning more. In the education system we put in a lot of effort and earn nothing in the end other than debt and regret for most. I was a victim who sacrificed three years of hard work with no employment in the end. Being a social media wizard, I was able to understand leverage pretty fast. Sometimes on a bad day I would work only an hour or two in a day and earn over £500. This result is impossible working in a supermarket or an average 9-5 job as it is limited with zero leverage. Now you understand why I hated the idea of having a job. I'm glad I was able to understand the power of leverage in a very short period of time as many people don't use leverage. Once again, this concept has been isolated in the education system. We have people leaving the universities and colleges, working hard physically, sometimes doing over time and still earning less and falling behind financially. To understand this concept in greater details I would advice you to read a book "*Retire Young Retire Rich*", by Robert Kiyosaki. He explains this powerful force in depth. In one of his chapter he mentioned this "*People with leverage have dominance over people with less leverage and if you understand the power of leverage you can beat big guys such as medical doctors, accountants, lawyers and anyone who has graduated from prestigious schools*" when I read that chapter the light bulbs went on. I started using leverage in everything I did.

Today, the internet is the biggest leverage people use. With the help of the internet, anyone can scale their business to a worldwide audience with very less effort promoting their products and services. The internet is at its prime. Let me give you an example, with the help of the internet, this book can be shipped to you in any part of the world as long as there's an internet connection and a good distribution channel. This is one of the reasons I decided to become an online marketer as there's unlimited leverage with millions to serve. This concept alone makes it clear why employees rarely get ahead financially or in life as they are limited both in choices and freedom. They are basically stuck in an environment they cannot excel from with somebody else controlling their life. You see what I mean.

While I'm still in the process of self-development and discovering the secrets of life, I noticed something. I keep seeing people reapplying and going back to universities to update their skill for a better chance of getting a high paying job and get further in debt. We both know one of the reasons why unemployment is rising is because technology and artificial intelligence are disrupting the job market, especially high paying jobs. Business owners can easily migrate a job to countries such as India, Philippines, Indonesia, North Korea at a very low cost than having to employ a fresh graduate with an MBA. With the advantage technology is providing employees are losing and entrepreneurs are winning. Business owners are more willing to invest their money in a system that is proven to work than having to employ graduates with an MBA, simply because people are expensive, they get tired, can sometimes be lazy and unpredictable. Whereas computers do the job 24hrs without getting tired, reliable and never complain about the weather. With the help of technology, business owners can just program what the computer has to do for them to make money and the computer does exactly what it's told even when the business owner is at sleep. I'm sure you would want that too. Universities and other education institutes are blind in this subject. The education system rarely mentions the impact of artificial intelligence in the job market. Many students are not aware of the fact that the job market is not like it used to be.

I've recently watched a video of a self-driving pizza delivery vehicle that Dominos could potentially introduce in the market. The vehicle processes everything from the local franchise to the customers address, all done electronically. I believe within the next 7 to 10 years delivery drivers could potentially be out of business with the power of technology, this may also affect construction workers, supermarket cashiers, book publishers, travel agents and manufacturer workers, again this is not a prophesy but it could happen. The world is changing rapidly, and we need to adapt to those changes. This means, we also need to become learning machine and constantly train our brain to recognize opportunities and become more valuable in the market with the help of technology, otherwise we'll become replaceable by somebody else or a robot. The education system does not reveal this to us. Many students perish as soon as they graduate due to lack of real knowledge. What we knew yesterday is no longer valuable with what we need to know tomorrow. The process is to learn, unlearn and relearn. Like, Charles Darwin said *"It is not the strongest of the species that survive, nor the most intelligent that survives. It is the one that is most adaptable to change"*. Becoming a learning machine and adapting to change that technology is providing into the market, is a huge competitive advantage that anyone can take to start and grow their business regardless of their background and succeed.

Talk with a Doctor

I often go to see my doctor every three months for regular check-ups and fitness purposes. I noticed that day he was absent, and I was appointed to see a different doctor instead. It was a young lady. I was surprised she could pronounce my full name, so I asked her if she spoke French or visited France before. She replied, *"no but I have a strong interest in languages"*. She was giving me all these amazing facts on how learning a language helps you connect with other people as well as understanding their culture and differences. She also mentioned how she has a passion for languages, learning three or four can be considered as an asset for anyone, she said. I was shocked hearing this from a doctor. I later then asked *"how come you decided to be a doctor even though you have a passion for languages"*. She said, *"I became a doctor to make my family proud, my parents only spoke about becoming a doctor while I was growing up and that's why I decided to become one, at that time we didn't know anything else"*. She even went on elaborating that her job is very challenging and wishes she could make more money as what she is currently getting is not enough. I then asked her if she would consider starting her own business part-time. This is what she said *"when I have time, I will eventually start a part-time business but right now, I'm so busy with the workload and other private occupation; don't get me wrong I really want to"*. I could see in her eyes she wanted to. I told her to find time even an hour or two in a day to focus on a part-time business. she replied back saying, *"I really should, I'm just waiting for the right time as there is so much required becoming a doctor"*. I said *"Good luck."* She finished with my check-up, and I was out the doctor's office.

Now and then every time I see her, she talks about how she still is interested in running her own part-time business but is waiting for the "right time" and her job is very demanding. It's the same excuse every time I see her. Unfortunately, "the right time" never comes, I believe she has even forgotten about starting her own business now. It's not her priority, yet she wants more money. This example applies to most people. A lot of people wait for the "perfect" time to do something in life. The ONLY problem with this is, "perfect" time never comes. You should aim to start where you are with what you have and adjust along the way. The road to success or financial freedom has never been a straight line, especially if most people want it. Even for those who inherited money from their parents, it's still not easy for them because they have to work to keep it. In fact, its often harder to keep money than to make money. Money itself doesn't make you rich, it has no value, it's what you do with it that makes the difference. What you know about money that makes the difference. You see, the road to financial freedom is a continuous learning process with a lot of ups and downs like the stock market. Some people might look at others and consider them as lucky without knowing the sacrifice that one had to put for something to work.

Many people avoid the process without realizing that it's the process that makes the person successful not the actual event. The education system doesn't teach us anything about the process and sacrifices that a person has to make to achieve a certain status or a goal. Students are becoming lazy to create and engage strategic thinking. When I mention the word "lazy", it doesn't necessarily imply that students are lazy to put in physical work. I simply use the word lazy in this context due to lack of resource management, this means failing to prepare and plan things strategically even with the use of the internet. Many students fail to understand the concept of self-education. They prefer going to universities, get in massive debt worth thousands of pounds and graduate with no job guarantee. Whereas, if they thought a little bit different, they could have simply bought a book at a cost of twenty to thirty pounds and get all the information they need to raise their curiosity, gain knowledge and build upon it. Do you see the huge difference? At the end of the day, the primary reason people go to university is to get information then turn it into practical knowledge. It's the same as reading a book and applying that knowledge into practice. This is what most lecturers are doing. Lecturers would buy a cheap book and use the same information to teach and get paid thousands. A smart student will question this and not follow the crowd.

CHAPTER 10

~VALUE~

There's a famous quote from Jim Rohn, a respected business philosopher that says "*formal education makes you a living; self-education makes you a fortune*". If you haven't read his book "*7 Strategies for Wealth & Happiness*" I would advice you to read it as it helped me understand the reason people fail and win the game of life, take responsibility, the importance of having a dream or a vision, how discipline attracts opportunity and the most important lesson called value that one brings into the market. In the educational system, I was taught that money makes the difference in the economy and society; everyone was focusing on the amount of money they will be making as soon as they graduate. The funny thing about this is that most students were chasing money when applying for jobs without even paying attention to the job title or the job specification, it was just sad to see how students were more interested in money than searching for real knowledge.

Doing online marketing and reading the book by Jim Rohn, I realized that it's not the money that makes the difference; it's the value that a person brings to the market. If you've noticed the word "value" has been mentioned quite a lot in this book; that is because value is a game changer. Creating value is what makes the difference in the economy; the rich add value into the system by creating jobs, providing housing, supporting the government, charitable donation and making a general impact into the world. That's why money follows their direction. On the other hand, the poor add little value to the market. Therefore they cannot attract or earn a lot of money. This concept does not just only apply in the economy or business but in life itself. For example, you're not going to date someone who doesn't add any sort of value into your life, are you? You wouldn't go to the movies without value, you wouldn't travel to work if there was no value involve, even reading this book! You wouldn't have gotten it if it wasn't for value. Value in the market place is king.

In school, we were never taught how to acquire in-demand skills for the marketplace or becoming indispensable in the market to serve a wide range of people. We spent hours memorizing planets, pacific oceans, world wars, which I believe is still important but just not relevant in the modern world. Let's take a look into sports. Have you ever wondered why Christiano Ronaldo, Floyd Mayweather, Tiger Woods and all these big names earn way more money than a university lecturer when education is supposed to be more important than sports and entertainment? The answer is simple, these guys have what we call in-demand skills and serve a wide range of people worldwide. They're indispensable in the market, very unique with productive value. It's very rare to find another player in their level and even if you did; it's not a crowded scene. Many people will pay just to see how these athletes perform in a competition, hence, their value in the market is estimated at a high cost. Looking at the education system we have hundreds or even thousands of lecturers who are teaching the same subject at colleges at the same level of speed. This means, the same modules, sometimes the same assignment and the same marking scheme. This gives students options to switch colleges or universities because they all provide the same information within the same system. Hence, they earn little because they are limited and easily replaceable with little market impact. In fact, teachers get sacked every day! Do you see what I mean? It's a shame they never taught us how to build skills that are in demand instead we learned about isosceles triangle and the Pacific Ocean.

Chapter 11

~From Hero to Zero~

As you're aware, I took a different path than most of my friends and family. My family respected people with Bachelors, MBA's, PhD's and all sort of academic qualifications. I respected entrepreneurs, people with integrity, character and courage. People who made something out of nothing, right out of thin air. As time went on, I and my partners decided to create a much more general online store, like Amazon; that's when everything went down the drain. In my opinion, the hardest part in business is dealing with people and not knowing the "how to do stuff". 8 months after doing online marketing we had problems, we couldn't make a sale. We tried every promotional tactic we thought of but there was nothing in return, I was annoyed. We had meetings after meetings to sort out the problem, but nothing worked. Because we went broad like Amazon and spent so much money testing product XYZ, there were no return. We should have kept a niche yet decided to go broad like Amazon. For that reason, we lost and closed down the business venture with Shopify drop shipping. But our dream never stopped there, we just stopped investing time in something that wasn't productive.

Both partners were very strong in business with tremendous moral support; I really do admire their courage and willpower. I struggled for months trying to figure out what to do next as my experience with Shopify didn't pay off well. Sometimes in life, we have to stop, re-evaluate what went wrong and start again. All I did in this phase was read books and wider up my knowledge. You see, it's a good advice to always have your cup half full and seek for more knowledge investing in your brain. I'm constantly looking for answers and will always be learning throughout my journey of life. If I'm not online watching educational videos on YouTube, I'm out networking or reading business books to then use the same strategy by tweaking it a little and applying it on my business. To me knowledge is a fuel that's needs refilling every time as we age, we should constantly seek information.

Weeks later, I went to see a friend and asked him to join me in this venture of becoming an entrepreneur. I told him I was up to something big and all he said was *"When I'm I going to get paid?" "how quick is it to make money?"*. When he said that I straightaway realized he wasn't the right partner to do business with. He wanted money, not the sacrifice it takes to build a business. I didn't see me again. Even though I made money in my first business, I had no cash flow coming in, and I was broke again, with a dream and a burning desire to change things. Being broke to me is not a problem staying broke is the problem, life is beautiful with unlimited wealth available to anyone willing to grab, so why stay broke? It doesn't make sense. Failing my first online business was a hard lesson to take in, but I managed to overcome it by moving on and letting it slide. I got ahead by failing first then learnt from my mistake, analyzed it and moved on. In the school system, once you fail, you're done. Which is wrong.

I was in the dark for months, but my mindset was strong. I realized that the education system doesn't teach us the power of having the right mindset to overcome failure. So many people want instant gratification without giving it time and when failure kicks in, the most logical way to think is to give up. You see, when you have the right mindset, no matter how long something can take; it will eventually fall in place. A focused mind can transform and make things happen; unfortunately, most people give up too early. This is why the gap between the rich and the poor is massive. The rich never give up, you shouldn't either. I believe we can accomplish anything with our two hands and our minds. But we have to be trained not just to sit there believing. The problem with many people is, they love inspirational quotes but don't act upon it. That's the problem. We have to train our minds and body to take action not just stimulate the mind. We have to change our habits and start developing successful habits. Society has done a good job blinding a lot of people believing that success is an event, material possessions or a lavish luxury lifestyle. That's very wrong. Your success is hidden in your consistent daily habits, success is not an event; success is a process.

Chapter 12

~Time to Take a Break~

I had a lot in my head, so I decided to take a break and travel to Congo, Kinshasa. What I love about my hometown is the food and the environment. Congo is a very rich country, yet its population is poor. Despite poverty, people there know how to live, they are naturally happy and very friendly, It's a mystery. If you're ever stressed or trying to figure out your next step in life try and visit the Congo, you'll feel like a King or Queen again. While I was on the plane flying for 9 hours, I noticed something. I noticed that the current school system doesn't teach us the value of time. Time is the most valuable asset in a human's life. Many people undervalue the value of time. We all have the same time as the people we admire, we just have to be wise with how we spend that time. So being on the plane, I realized the importance of time as my destination was determined by time. Time is life. And the more you waste time, the more you waste life.

Most time, if you just observe you will see that most people believe that they're immortal and party in their youth non-stop without realizing that time is limited. Some postpone what they should have done today with the idea of having a lot of time. The only problem with this is those same people will turn forty or fifty doing the job they hate to realize later how important time is. I'm not writing to judge anyone because we live in the world where anyone can do what they want. However, we just have to be careful with how we spend our time. There's a woman I once met, she was a security guard. Out of curiosity, I asked her how come she ended up doing security. She told me when she was a lot younger, all she did was party from city to city, she moved to Spain and got married. 15 years later she got divorced, and now there's no one to employ her because she lacks in-demand skills for the market. It's a sad story. She found herself in that situation all this because she never understood the value of time. Although, it's never too late to reinvent herself but its too late to start all over again as time has passed. She's now 49.

Many people trade their time for money, they go to university, find a job and live life in a box working their entire life for money. They become a product of the environment and for many, they never chose to be in that position but because they had no guidance, made poor decisions repetitively with little to no knowledge of the real world; they ended up sacrificing their precious time for little nuggets. And time passes on. If they were wise enough to realize that time is by far more important than money, they would have taken action by finding the right mentors for guidance, seek real knowledge and be in control of their life. The thing is, when you trade your time for money you will be standing where you don't want to be. I wish they taught me this in school. I would have taken action much earlier.

After such a long journey, I finally arrived in Kinshasa to get my head right and focus on my next step in life. It was such a nice feeling seeing the family and friends after a long time. After a week, I was surfing throughout the internet as usual and saw another advert on YouTube. This time it was a social media mogul advertising his course. Because I was already aware of online marketing and social media, I knew he wasn't bullshitting. He's advert was vibrant and captivating, I just had to believe him; there were no cynicism, I was just hooked. The guy said *"if you want to be rich or make money, you have to be able to read trends and get in quickly before everyone. We live in a world where opportunities fly left and right, but most people fail to recognize it, and there are three reasons for that. 1. they're skeptical 2. They haven't been trained to recognize the opportunity and 3. They are at sleep"*. He added again by saying *"there's an opportunity knocking right now in front of you, sometimes you just need to have a little faith and believe in yourself. This course will work, the sooner you enter the sooner you win and I hope you win"*. That was the end. It just felt like he was talking to me directly. I felt it. I quickly did some research about the guy before buying the course. I found out he didn't grow up with much, but the internet precisely social media changed his life forever. This guy makes over $300,000 a day!

Sometimes a million in an hour! It was a big opportunity and I couldn't resist, I bought the program straight away. Because I was in Africa, with family and friends, I wanted to find a place where I can concentrate and start this new venture. I decided to travel back to Europe and train myself. Now a new path was discovered with light at the end of the tunnel.

Chapter 13

~Back to Europe~

We're soon approaching the end of our conversation. If you understand the core of this book you will definitely understand that we live in the information age, and not the old industrial age where people had to work hard physically to get ahead in life. We live in the generation where information travel so fast; almost as the same speed of light. All these skills and information I've acquired was because of the internet. We don't necessarily have to go to school or university to learn, everything is right in front of us and we can make money pretty fast with the internet connection. I don't want you to sleep in this opportunity as trends come and go. Now is the best time to take action to either start your own part-time business or help other businesses generate cash. I believe every business that want to grow and expand will need to learn how to use social media. Failing to adapt to this trend may result in catastrophe. For instance, just to name a few names, Nokia, Blockbuster, Sears, Kodak and ToysRUs failed to adapt to this shift of evolving their online presence when the internet was booming and using social media marketing to promote their services. So, for that reason, they all faced difficulties and ended up bankrupt. Don't get me wrong some companies might still be in business, but the market now is highly competitive with Instagram, Netflix, Amazon and online drop shipping available. If they took advantage of evolving their online presence back then, surely it would have been a different story. And there's more to come if companies fail to learn the use of E-commerce and social media marketing. Especially big companies.

I certainly believe this is the best opportunity for young entrepreneurs to help businesses increase their sales with the use of social media as most business owners have limited knowledge of how to navigate with social media. The average business owner is 50 years old. Honestly speaking, do you really think an average 50-year-old would sit down and start uploading pictures on Instagram promoting their products or services online? or focus on growing their business offline? it's pretty obvious, business owners are busy people! They are busy signing contracts, employing staff, dealing with taxes, customer complaints as well as taking care of their home and other private occupation. Social media will be the last thing on their mind. Business owners have good management skills, they're good doing business but have limited skills with social media, they need our help! So, this is such an opportunity for us young entrepreneurs to learn social media and provide a lot of value out of it because the internet is the new way of getting new customers. Unfortunately, since most people are trained to look for jobs they don't recognize this opportunity. The school system on the other hand has never taught us how to see the future, but instead we learn history not the future.

Let me state a crucial point, no matter what happens with the economy or the stock market, people will still buy products online. There's a reason why Jeff Bezos, Amazon CEO is the richest man in the world; people prefer buying online. If you're a business owner, the longer you wait to sell online the harder is going to be as more and more people have started selling their products online using Amazon, Shopify and click funnels. It's not too late as the trend is still running. Understanding this concept alone is such a competitive advantage as there are very less to zero overhead costs with online selling. Remember with online selling there are no human contact involve as everything is done electronically, it doesn't matter if you're old, young, black, white, tall, short, fat, skinny; it works! E-commerce is a system doing the job for you, it will do exactly what you've programmed it to do. Even in recession e-commerce will rise as people will always want to buy online regardless of what happens, we're lazy like that. People prefer items coming to them because its less effort. Now imagine if you're a business owner and have a strong online presence, you will sleep well at night.

I finally landed back in Birmingham, United Kingdom and started learning. I spent four to six months mastering social media and understanding the world behind Facebook, YouTube, Twitter and Instagram. It was such an intense course that I had to block myself from socializing with family and close friends but it was definitely worth it. While I was doing the course, I soon realized that the course had a lot of creativity involved with many different ideas and understanding from students who also purchased the course, they were no right or wrong answers. In school or university, we are not taught how to think independently; we are taught how to think the teacher's way. Independent thinking forces you to expand your vision and finding a way to make things happen. In the education system, teachers tend to inject their reality into our lives, and we just accept it without having to question. I believe, you shouldn't just accept what anyone is telling you unless you want to be like that person. I went to the university studying business by a person who never ran a business and was handed a business degree. Wow! When you're young and naïve, you really do believe anything people say with "hope" something works. I strongly believe if you want to learn how to do something, you should try and study it under a person who has done what you want to achieve or trying to achieve. To me, this concept is more reasonable and it's proven to work.

During the course, I discovered that most people live their entire life below their full potential. Let me explain, the majority of people worldwide, including the dumbest person you know have a good idea. The only difference with them and people that make it is, they don't know how to do it; that's one of the aspects what blocks most people to achieve their dream. They don't know how to do what they know. Most people fear change or judgement from other people, this again is a major issue that blocks them from exploring the beauty of life. what a shame. This is my first book in the market; do you really think opinions or judgements from other people matter? Of course not. Even if I sold 10 to 10 million copies of this book, it doesn't matter as I'm on the journey to improve my products and services and serve the world by giving out information. If we look into technology, we will see that Apple still innovate its products and they do it really well. We went from iPhone (1st generation) to iPhone XS, and there's still more to come. What I'm illustrating here is we should try new things and always seek ways to improve what we're currently doing. When you keep improving your services, people will naturally keep coming back to you because us humans, we love new and exciting products that fulfill the needs. Your first idea shouldn't be your last idea. Remember your only limit in this world is yourself, not the government, not your boss, not your husband, not your wife or children but YOU! I'm not just saying that for superficial reason or to sound nice, it's the truth. I wish they taught us this in school.

In my opinion, I honestly believe the education system is designed for us live an average life or below average with no cutting-edge tools. This could come across as harsh. Excuse me if you're offended but it's the truth. Once again, this does not apply to everyone and I'm not saying you shouldn't go to school or school is bad for you closed minded people. School is the foundation of education but if you want to live an extraordinary life, believe me, school is not the way. People don't often realize this until they've turned a certain age only to realise that life has already passed them by. If you have children or relatives in the current school system, don't just allow school to educate them while you're at work to make ends meet. In my humble opinion I believe if a person only focuses on school or university and fails to discover their true potential, life will get harder because there's no guarantee with the education system. Think about it, if there are thousands of people studying exactly the same degree as you or your relative what makes you guys different and what are the chances of beating the odds? Think about that for a few minutes.

Even if you graduate from top university, what's the probability of you becoming exceptional? Take responsibility to self-educate and teach your child your way of learning. Ask them questions, get to know them and seek the genius hidden inside them. You never know who they'll turn out to be with good guidance and better education from home. Schools or colleges will not educate your child for you. School teachers also have a family to take care of, they only go to schools to do their job. If they find another better job opportunity elsewhere they will happily leave one job to the next. So please, let us take care of our children by educating them our way not the modern society way. If you're already doing so, congratulations!

Chapter 14

~It Finally Paid Off Once Again~

After being trained and mastering social media marketing, I've managed to build a social media agency with a mission of helping local businesses increase their sales using online marketing. What I do is install a funnel system that drives social media users to my client's website and then turn these potential users into customers. First, I provide a lot of content to why customers should use a particular product or service and the person watching will end up buying. Just to keep things clear, there's a process to it; people don't just buy stuff like magic. But it works, you're the evidence that online selling works, you've got the book.

    We can also help international business owners in any niche you can think of. The same principle applies worldwide, all we need to do to increase your business sales using social media is internet connection, a mobile phone and a laptop. With the internet connection, I and my team will help your business increase sales by simply targeting people in your local area the product you offer and the benefit of using your product. After being well advertised, these people will turn into customers. If you're a business owner and want to increase revenue to have the freedom your heart desire, we can help you. Please feel free to visit our website at www.fastlanemarketing.co.uk or send us an email at Fastlanemarketing10@gmail.com. Your inquiry will come directly to me the CEO of the company. We offer a FREE business consultation to our potential clients where we evaluate their website and social media outlets. If you're a perfect fit for our company, we will then send you a package to help you choose from. All this can be done in less than 48hrs. Our aim is to seek ways and methods to make our clients lives easier by handling their weakness and turning it into strength.

Conclusion

Phew!! We have finally approached the end of our conversation. This book was written to expose some truths behind the education system and encourage readers to acquire social media skillsets and help business owners increase revenue. The school system is failing a lot of people even those highly educated. Many people are kept in the dark because of what they've been taught in school. For instance, most people are told that getting into debt is a bad idea because school never taught us the difference between good debt and bad debt. There are good debt and bad debt. Good debt enriches your life but it takes a lot of education to understand this concept and bad debt make you a modern slave, that's very easy to get in. Unfortunately, most people only see the bad not the good. We are taught to accept whatever is thrown at us without having to question why, that's why I never liked school. School prepares you to obey anything your boss tells you including what to do with your money once you get paid. This is usually done by influencing employees to invest in company shares, stock market or any investment the employee doesn't have control. This sort of manipulation is what causes a lot of people to live in darkness with little to zero financial education. Just because someone is giving you advice, it does not mean they know what they are talking about.

When you're destined to be a worker, your whole life is to work and protect the assets for the rich. I'm not here to tell you what is right or wrong because some people love their job, but if you want to live an exceptional life beyond 9-5; learn how to fish. I believe we should teach a man how to fish than having to give him fish. Giving fish to a man promotes laziness, and he will keep coming back asking for more, whereas teaching him how to fish will change his life forever and those around him. To me, this makes sense than having to look for salvation from an individual. Understand that money is still not the answer and people shouldn't chase money but learn to attract it. I like what Robert Kiyosaki once said *"money is just an opinion"* I totally agree with it. What you think of money becomes your reality of money. If you think money is "evil" you've already lost. Money has no face and is an illusion. Real money is knowledge, and the ability to transform information and then being able create value for others is what money is. Paper money has zero value. There's a biblical quote that I like in the book of Hosea 4:6 that states *"my people perish for lack of knowledge"*. This is true because those who will succeed in years to come are the people who can adapt to change with the speed of the technology, people who are aware of their surroundings and always educating themselves to get better by day as well as setting higher goals to bring out the giant in them. Those are the people who will inherit the earth.

In years to come, I believe the future of education will be based on the Internet. Many colleges and universities will face a hard time if they choose not to endorse their courses online or implement live streaming, again this is not a prophecy. Online education is rising and could potentially be the most profitable and cutting-edge tool way of learning. This is because students will begin to get taught by successful professors who practise what they preach in any subject of their choice. The internet is the new leverage in education as it's attracting successful professions across the world teaching unlimited numbers of students globally. Many people prefer picking up a skill much quicker rather than having to wait three to four years at university with nothing but "hope" for a job. Furthermore, a wide range of students would prefer to watch an online course at home than having to drive two hours for a seminar. We all hate traffic!

Online self-education will be different, and students will have access to giants who dominate industries teaching them at their own comfort. This mean they can watch them in bed, on the beach, in the toilet, anywhere and at any time with just the internet connection. Even at 2 am with a refund guarantee that universities do NOT provide. We now have access to receive a much higher quality of education at very low cost comparing with what colleges or universities is currently charging. The first time in human kind history! I hope this book has provided you with some sort of value, please do not read this book and just forget about it. I want you to take action in your dream. Remember there's always hope for those who live. Have little bit of faith. Just little ...

Thanks for picking up this book.

Your servant, *Romeo Olivier.*

You can follow me on Snapchat: ItsRomeo_06
Instagram: Romeo.Olivierr
Facebook: Romeo Olivier

www.ingramcontent.com/pod-product-compliance
Lightning Source LLC
Chambersburg PA
CBHW031536210526
45464CB00003B/1040